BEHIND THE BEYOND

STEPHEN LEACOCK

THE PROLOGUE

BEHIND THE BEYOND

AND OTHER CONTRIBUTIONS TO HUMAN KNOWLEDGE

BY STEPHEN LEACOCK

AUTHOR OF "NONSENSE NOVELS," "LITERARY LAPSES," "SUNSHINE SKETCHES," ETC.

ILLUSTRATED BY A. H. FISH

NEW YORK: JOHN LANE COMPANY
LONDON: JOHN LANE, THE BODLEY HEAD
TORONTO: BELL & COCKBURN. MCMXIII

CONTENTS

ILLUSTRATIONS

I

BEHIND THE BEYOND

**A MODERN PROBLEM PLAY IN THREE ACTS AND TWO DRINKS*

**In Intimate Collaboration with Moreorless Muddleink, Airman Sodaman, Yibson Yibsen, Yawn Yawnson, Jack Jornson and Many Others.*

Act I.—Behind the Beyond

THE curtain rises, disclosing the ushers of the theater still moving up and down the aisles. Cries of "Program!" "Program!" are heard. There is a buzz of brilliant conversation, illuminated with flashes of opera glasses and the rattle of expensive jewelry.

Then suddenly, almost unexpectedly, in fact just as if done, so to speak, by machinery, the lights all over the theater, except on the stage, are extinguished. Absolute silence falls. Here and there is heard the crackle of a shirt front. But there is no other sound.

In this expectant hush, a man in a check tweed suit walks on the stage: only one man, one single man. Because if he had been accompanied by a chorus, that would have been a burlesque; if four citizens in togas had been with him, that would have been Shakespeare;

if two Russian soldiers had walked after him, that would have been melodrama. But this is none of these. This is a problem play. So he steps in alone, all alone, and with that absolute finish of step, that ability to walk as if,—how can one express it?—as if he were walking, that betrays the finished actor.

He has, in fact, barely had time to lay down his silk hat, when he is completely betrayed. You can see that he is a finished actor—finished about fifteen years ago. He lays the hat, hollow side up, on the silk hat table on the stage right center—bearing north, northeast, half a point west from the red mica fire on the stage which warms the theater.

All this is done very, very quietly, very impressively. No one in the theater has ever seen a man lay a silk hat on a table before, and so there is a breathless hush. Then he takes off his gloves, one by one, *not* two or three at a time, and lays them in his hat. The expectancy is almost painful. If he had thrown his gloves into the mica fire it would have been a relief. But he doesn't.

The Curtain rises.

The man on the stage picks up a pile of letters from the letter department of the hat table. There are a great many of these letters, because all his business correspondence, as well as his private letters, are sent here by the General Post Office. Getting his letters in this way at night, he is able to read them like lightning. Some of them he merely holds upside down for a fraction of a second.

Then at last he speaks. It has become absolutely necessary or he wouldn't do it. "So—Sao Paolo risen two—hum—Rio Tinto down again—Moreby anxious, 'better sell for half a million sterling'—hum . . ."

(Did you hear that? Half a million sterling and he takes it just as quietly as that. And it isn't really in the play either. Sao Paolo and Rio Tinto just come in to let you know the sort of man you're dealing with.)

"Lady Gathorne—dinner—Thursday the ninth—lunch with the Ambassador—Friday the tenth."

(And mind you even this is just patter. The

Ambassador doesn't come into the play either. He and Lady Gathorne are just put in to let the people in the cheaper seats know the kind of thing they're up against.)

Then the man steps across the stage and presses a button. A bell rings. Even before it has finished ringing, nay, just before it begins to ring, a cardboard door swings aside and a valet enters. You can tell he is a valet because he is dressed in the usual home dress of a stage valet.

He says, "Did you ring, Sir John?"

There is a rustle of programs all over the house. You can hear a buzz of voices say, "He's Sir John Trevor." They're all on to him.

When the valet says, "Did you ring, Sir John," he ought to answer, "No, I merely knocked the bell over to see how it would sound," but he misses it and doesn't say it.

"Has her ladyship come home?"

"Yes, Sir John."

"Has any one been here?"

"Mr. Harding, Sir John."

"Any one else?"

"No, Sir John."

"Very good."

The valet bows and goes out of the cardboard door, and everybody in the theater, or at least everybody in the seats worth over a dollar, knows that there's something strange in the relations of Lady Trevor and Mr. Harding. You notice—Mr. Harding was there and no one else was there. That's enough in a problem play.

The double door at the back of the stage, used only by the principal characters, is opened and Lady Cicely Trevor enters. She is young and very beautiful, and wears a droopy hat and long slinky clothes which she drags across the stage. She throws down her feather hat and her crêpe de what-you-call-it boa on the boa stand. Later on the valet comes in and gathers them up. He is always gathering up things like this on the stage—hats and boas and walking sticks thrown away by the actors,—but nobody notices him. They are his perquisites.

Sir John says to Lady Cicely, "Shall I ring for tea?"

And Lady Cicely says, "Thanks. No," in a weary tone.

This shows that they are the kind of people who can have tea at any time. All through a problem play it is understood that any of the characters may ring for tea and get it. Tea in a problem play is the same as whisky in a melodrama.

Then there ensues a dialogue to this effect: Sir John asks Lady Cicely if she has been out. He might almost have guessed it from her coming in in a hat and cloak, but Sir John is an English baronet.

Lady Cicely says, "Yes, the usual round," and distributes a few details about Duchesses and Princesses, for the general good of the audience.

Then Lady Cicely says to Sir John, "You are going out?"

"Yes, immediately."

"To the *House,* I suppose."

This is very impressive. It doesn't mean, as

you might think, the Workhouse, or the White House, or the Station House, or the Bon Marché. It is the name given by people of Lady Cicely's class to the House of Commons.

"Yes. I am extremely sorry. I had hoped I might ask to go with you to the opera. I fear it is impossible—an important sitting—the Ministers will bring down the papers—the Kafoonistan business. The House will probably divide in committee. Gatherson will ask a question. We must stop it at all costs. The fate of the party hangs on it."

Sir John has risen. His manner has changed. His look is altered. You can see him alter it. It is now that of a statesman. The technical details given above have gone to his head. He can't stop.

He goes on: "They will force a closure on the second reading, go into committee, come out of it again, redivide, subdivide and force us to bring down the estimates."

While Sir John speaks, Lady Cicely's manner has been that of utter weariness. She has picked up the London *Times* and thrown it aside; taken up a copy of *Punch* and let it fall with a thud to the floor, looked idly at a piece of music and decided, evidently, *not* to sing it. Sir John runs out of technical terms and stops.

The dialogue has clearly brought out the following points: Sir John is in the House of Commons. Lady Cicely is not. Sir John is twenty-five years older than Lady Cicely. He doesn't see—isn't he a fool, when everybody in the gallery can see it?—that his parliamentary work is meaningless to her, that her life is insufficient. That's it. Lady Cicely is being "starved." All that she has is money, position, clothes, and jewelry. These things starve any woman. They cramp her. That's what makes problem plays.

Lady Cicely speaks, very quietly, "Are you taking Mr. Harding with you?"

"Why?"

"Nothing. I thought perhaps I might ask him to take me to the opera. Puffi is to sing."

"Do, pray do. Take Harding with you by all means. Poor boy, do take him with you."

Sir John pauses. He looks at Lady Cicely

very quietly for a moment. He goes on with a slight change in his voice.

"Do you know, Cicely, I've been rather troubled about Harding lately. There's something the matter with the boy, something wrong."

"Yes?"

"He seems abstracted, moody—I think, in fact I'm sure that the boy is in love."

"Yes?"

Lady Cicely has turned slightly pale. The weariness is out of her manner.

"Trust the instinct of an old man, my dear. There's a woman in it. We old parliamentary hands are very shrewd, you know, even in these things. Some one is playing the devil with Jack—with Harding."

Sir John is now putting on his gloves again and gathering up his parliamentary papers from the parliamentary paper stand on the left.

He cannot see the change in Lady Cicely's face. He is not meant to see it. But even the little girls in the tenth row of the gallery are wise.

He goes on. "Talk to Harding. Get it out of him. You women can do these things. Find out what the trouble is and let me know. I must help him." (A pause. Sir John is speaking almost to himself—and the gallery.) "I promised his mother when she sent him home, sent him to England, that I would."

Lady Cicely speaks. "You knew Mr. Harding's mother very well?"

Sir John: "Very well."

"That was long ago, wasn't it?"

"Long ago."

"Was she married then?"

"No, not then."

"Here in London?"

"Yes, in London. I was only a barrister then with my way to make and she a famous beauty." (Sir John is speaking with a forced levity that doesn't deceive even the ushers.) "She married Harding of the Guards. They went to India. And there he spent her fortune—and broke her heart." Sir John sighs.

"You have seen her since?"

"Never."

"She has never written you?"

"Only once. She sent her boy home and wrote to me for help. That was how I took him as my secretary."

"And that was why he came to us in Italy two years ago, just after our marriage."

"Yes, that was why."

"Does Mr. Harding know?"

"Know what?"

"That you—knew his mother?"

Sir John shakes his head. "I have never talked with him about his mother's early life."

The stage clock on the mantelpiece begins to strike. Sir John lets it strike up to four or five, and then says, "There, eight o'clock. I must go. I shall be late at the House. Good-by."

He moves over to Lady Cicely and kisses her. There is softness in his manner—such softness that he forgets the bundle of parliamentary papers that he had laid down. Everybody can see that he has forgotten them. They were right there under his very eye.

Sir John goes out.

Lady Cicely stands looking fixedly at the fire. She speaks out loud to herself. "How his voice changed—twenty-five years ago—so long as that—I wonder if Jack knows."

There is heard the ring of a bell off the stage. The valet enters.

"Mr. Harding is downstairs, my lady."

"Show him up, Ransome."

A moment later Mr. Harding enters. He is a narrow young man in a frock coat. His face is weak. It has to be. Mr. Harding is meant to typify weakness. Lady Cicely walks straight to him. She puts her two hands on his shoulders and looks right into his face.

"MY DARLING," she says. Just like that. In capital letters. You can feel the thrill of it run through the orchestra chairs. All the audience look at Mr. Harding, some with opera glasses, others with eyeglasses on sticks. They can see that he is just the sort of ineffectual young man that a starved woman in a problem play goes mad over.

Lady Cicely repeats "My darling" several times. Mr. Harding says "Hush," and tries to disengage himself. She won't let him. He offers to ring for tea. She won't have any. "Oh, Jack," she says. "I can't go on any longer. I can't. When first you loved me, I thought I could. But I can't. It throttles me here—this house, this life, everything——" She has drawn him to a sofa and has sunk down in a wave at his feet. "Do you remember, Jack, when first you came, in Italy, that night, at Amalfi, when we sat on the piazza of the palazzo?" She is looking rapturously into his face.

Mr. Harding says that he does.

"And that day at Fiesole among the orange trees, and Pisa and the Capello de Terisa and the Mona Lisa—Oh, Jack, take me away from all this, take me to the Riviera, among the contadini, where we can stand together with my head on your shoulder just as we did in the Duomo at Milano, or on the piaggia at Verona. Take me to Corfu, to the Campo Santo, to Civita Vecchia, to Para Noia—anywhere——"

Mr. Harding, smothered with her kisses, says, "My dearest, I will, I will." Any man in the audience would do as much. They'd take her to Honolulu.

While she is speaking, Sir John's voice had been heard off the stage. "No, thank you, Ransome, I'll get them myself, I know just where I left them." Sir John enters hurriedly, advances and picks up his papers on the table—turns—and stands——

He sees his wife's attitude and hears her say "Riviera, Amalfi, Orangieri, Contadini and Capello Santo." It is enough. He drops his parliamentary papers. They fall against the fire irons with a crash. These in falling upset a small table with one leg. The ball of wool that is on it falls to the floor. The noise of this disturbs the lovers.

They turn. All three look at one another. For a moment they make a motion as if to ring for tea. Then they stand petrified.

"You!" gasps Lady Cicely. She does this awfully well. Everybody says afterward that it was just splendid when she said "You."

Sir John stands gazing in horror. "Him!

My God! He!" Mr. Harding says nothing. He looks very weak.

Lady Cicely unpetrifies first.

She breaks out, speaking through her nostrils. "Yes, I love him, I love him. I'm not ashamed of it. What right have you to deny it me? You gave me nothing. You made me a chattel, a thing——"

You can feel the rustle of indignation through the house at this. To make a woman a thing is the crowning horror of a problem play.

"You starved me here. You throttled me." Lady Cicely takes herself by the neck and throttles herself a little to show how.

"You smothered me. I couldn't breathe—and now I'm going, do you hear, going away, to life, to love, behind the beyond!" She gathers up Mr. Harding (practically) and carries him passionately away. He looks back weakly as he goes.

Sir John has sunk down upon a chair. His face is set.

"Jack," he mutters, "my God, Jack!"

As he sits there, the valet enters with a telegram on a tray.

"A telegram, Sir John."

Sir John (dazed and trying to collect himself), "What?"

"A telegram, sir,—a cablegram."

Sir John takes it, opens it and reads aloud:

"He is dead. My duty is ended. I am coming home—Margaret Harding."

"Margaret coming home. It only needed that—my God."

. . . .

As he says it, the curtain falls.

The lights flick up. There is a great burst of applause. The curtain rises and falls. Lady Cicely and Mr. Harding and Sir John all come out and bow charmingly. There is no trace of worry on their faces, and they hold one another's hands. Then the curtain falls and the orchestra breaks out into a Winter Garden waltz. The boxes buzz with discussion. Some of the people think that Lady Cicely is right in claiming the right to realize herself: others think that before realizing herself she should have developed herself. Others ask indignantly how she could know herself if her husband refused to let her be herself. But everybody feels that the subject is a delicious one.

Those of the people who have seen the play before very kindly explain how it ends, so as to help the rest to enjoy it. But the more serious-minded of the men have risen, very gently, and are sneaking up the aisles. Their expression is stamped with deep thought as if pondering over the play. But their step is as that of leopards on the march, and no one is deceived as to their purpose.

The music continues. The discussion goes on.

The leopards come stealing back. The orchestra boils over in a cadence and stops. The theater is darkened again. The footlights come on with a flash. The curtain silently lifts, and it is—

Act II.—Six Months Later

THE programs rustle. The people look to see where it is. And they find that it is "An Apartment in Paris." Notice that this place which is used in every problem play is just called *An Apartment.* It is not called Mr. Harding's Apartment, or an Apartment for which Mr. Harding pays the Rent. Not a bit. It is just an Apartment. Even if it were "A Apartment" it would feel easier. But *"An Apartment"!!* The very words give the audience a delicious shiver of uncomfortableness.

When the curtain rises it discloses a French maid moving about the stage in four-dollar silk stockings. She is setting things on a little table, evidently for supper. She explains this in French as she does it, so as to make it clear.

"*Bon! la serviette de monsieur! bon! la serviette de madame, bien—du champagne, bon! langouste aux champignons, bien, bon.*—" This is all the French she knows, poor little thing,

Their expression is stamped with deep thought.

but *langouste aux champignons* beats the audience, so she is all right.

Anyway, this supper scene has to come in. It is symbolical. You can't really show Amalfi and Fiesole and the orange trees, so this kind of supper takes their place.

As the maid moves about there is a loud knock at the cardboard door of the apartment. A man in official clothes sticks his head in. He is evidently a postal special messenger because he is all in postal attire with a postal glazed hat.

"Monsieur Arrding?" he says.

"*Oui.*"

"*Bon! Une lettre.*"

"*Merci, monsieur.*" He goes out. The audience feel a thrill of pride at having learned French and being able to follow the intense realism of this dialogue. The maid lays the letter on the supper table.

Just as she does it the door opens and there enter Mr. Harding and Lady Cicely. Yes, them. Both of them. The audience catches it like a flash. They *live* here.

Lady Cicely throws aside her cloak. There is great gaiety in her manner. Her face is paler. There is a bright spot in each cheek. Her eyes are very bright.

There follows the well-known supper scene. Lady Cicely is very gay. She pours champagne into Mr. Harding's glass. They both drink from it. She asks him if he is a happy boy now. He says he is. She runs her fingers through his hair. He kisses her on the bare shoulder. This is also symbolic.

Lady Cicely rattles on about Amalfi and Fiesole. She asks Mr. Harding if he remembers that night in the olive trees at Santa Clara, with just one thrush singing in the night sky. He says he does. He remembers the very thrush. You can see from the talk that they have been all over Baedeker's guide to the Adriatic.

At times Lady Cicely's animation breaks. She falls into a fit of coughing and presses her hand to her side. Mr. Harding looks at her apprehensively. She says, "It is nothing, silly

He kisses her on the bare shoulder.

boy, it will be gone in a moment." It is only because she is so happy.

Then, quite suddenly, she breaks down and falls at Mr. Harding's knees.

"Oh, Jack, Jack, I can't stand it! I can't stand it any longer. It is choking me!"

"My darling, what is it?"

"This, all this, it is choking me—this apartment, these pictures, the French maid, all of it. I can't stand it. I'm being suffocated. Oh, Jack, take me away—take me somewhere where it is quiet, take me to Norway to the great solemn hills and the fjords——"

Then suddenly Mr. Harding sees the letter in its light blue envelope lying on the supper table. It has been lying right beside him for ten minutes. Everybody in the theater could see it and was getting uncomfortable about it. He clutches it and tears it open. There is a hunted look in his face as he reads.

"What is it?"

"My mother—good God, she is coming. She

is at the Bristol and is coming here. What can I do?"

Lady Cicely is quiet now.

"Does she know?"

"Nothing, nothing."

"How did she find you?"

"I don't know. I can't imagine. I knew when I saw in the papers that my father was dead that she would come home. But I kept back the address. I told the solicitors, curse them, to keep it secret."

Mr. Harding paces the stage giving an imitation of a weak man trapped. He keeps muttering, "What can I do?"

Lady Cicely speaks very firmly and proudly. "Jack."

"What?"

"There is only one thing to do. Tell her."

Mr. Harding, aghast, "Tell her?"

"Yes, tell her about our love, about everything. I am not ashamed. Let her judge me."

Mr. Harding sinks into a chair. He keeps shivering and saying, "I tell you, I can't; I can't. She wouldn't understand." The letter is fluttering in his hand. His face is contemptible. He does it splendidly. Lady Cicely picks the letter from his hand. She reads it aloud, her eyes widening as she reads:

HOTEL BRISTOL, PARIS.

MY DARLING BOY:

I have found you at last—why have you sought to avoid me? God grant there is nothing wrong. He is dead, the man I taught you to call your father, and I can tell you all now. I am coming to you this instant.

MARGARET HARDING.

Lady Cicely reads, her eyes widen and her voice chokes with horror.

She advances to him and grips his hand. "What does it mean, Jack, tell me what does it mean?"

"Good God, Cicely, don't speak like that."

"This—these lines—about your father."

"I don't know what it means—I don't care—I hated him, the brute. I'm glad he's dead. I don't care for that. But she's coming here, any minute, and I can't face it."

Lady Cicely, more quietly, "Jack, tell me,

did my—did Sir John Trevor ever talk to you about your father?"

"No. He never spoke of him."

"Did he know him?"

"Yes—I think so—long ago. But they were enemies—Trevor challenged him to a duel—over some woman—and he wouldn't fight—the cur."

Lady Cicely (dazed and aghast)—"I—understand—it—now." She recovers herself and speaks quickly.

"Listen. There is time yet. Go to the hotel. Go at once. Tell your mother nothing. Nothing, you *understand.* Keep her from coming here. Anything, but not that. Ernestine,"—She calls to the maid who reappears for a second—"a taxi—at once."

She hurriedly gets Harding's hat and coat. The stage is full of bustle. There is a great sense of hurry. The audience are in an agony for fear Ernestine is too slow, or calls a four-wheel cab by mistake. If the play is really well put on, you can presently hear the taxi buzzing outside. Mr. Harding goes to kiss

Lady Cicely. She puts him from her in horror and hastens him out.

She calls the maid. "Ernestine, quick, put my things, anything, into a valise."

"Madame is going away!"

"Yes, yes, at once."

"Madame will not eat?"

"No, no."

"Madame will not first rest?" (The slow comprehension of these French maids is something exasperating.) "Madame will not await monsieur?

"Madame will not first eat, nor drink—no? Madame will not sleep?"

"No, no—quick, Ernestine. Bring me what I want. Summon a fiacre. I shall be ready in a moment." Lady Cicely passes through a side door into an inner room.

She is scarcely gone when Mrs. Harding enters. She is a woman about forty-five, still very beautiful. She is dressed in deep black.

(The play is now moving very fast. You have to sit tight to follow it all.)

She speaks to Ernestine. "Is this Mr. Harding's apartment?"

"Yes, madame."

"Is he here?" She looks about her.

"No, madame, he is gone this moment in a taxi—to the Hotel Bristol, I heard him say."

Mrs. Harding, faltering. "Is—any one—here?"

"No, madame, no one—milady was here a moment ago. She, too, has gone out." (This is a lie but of course the maid is a French maid.)

"Then it is true—there is some one——" She is just saying this when the bell rings, the door opens and there enters—Sir John Trevor.

"You!" says Mrs. Harding.

"I am too late!" gasps Sir John.

She goes to him tremblingly—"After all these years," she says.

"It is a long time."

"You have not changed."

She has taken his hands and is looking into his face, and she goes on speaking. "I have thought of you so often in all these bitter years

—it sustained me even at the worst—and I knew, John, that it was for my sake that you had never married——"

Then, as she goes on talking, the audience realize with a thrill that Mrs. Harding does not know that Sir John married two years ago, that she has come home, as she thought, to the man who loved her, and, more than that, they get another thrill when they realize that Lady Cicely is learning it too. She has pushed the door half open and is standing there unseen, listening. She wears a hat and cloak; there is a folded letter in her hand—her eyes are wide. Mrs. Harding continues:

"And now, John, I want your help, only you can help me, you are so strong—my Jack, I must save him." She looks about the room. Something seems to overcome her. "Oh, John, this place—his being here like this—it seems a judgment on us."

The audience are getting it fast now. And when Mrs. Harding speaks of "our awful moment of folly," "the retribution of our own sins," they grasp it and shiver with the luxury of it.

After that when Mrs. Harding says: "Our wretched boy, we must save him,"—they all know why she says "our."

She goes on more calmly. "I realized. I knew—he is not alone here."

Sir John's voice is quiet, almost hollow. "He is not alone."

"But this woman—can you not deal with her—persuade her—beg her for my sake—bribe her to leave my boy?"

Lady Cicely steps out. "There is no bribe needed. I am going. If I have wronged him, and you, it shall be atoned."

Sir John has given no sign. He is standing stunned. She turns to him. "I have heard and know now. I cannot ask for pity. But when I am gone—when it is over—I want you to give him this letter—and I want you, you two, to—to be as if I had never lived."

She lays the letter in his hand. Then without a sign, Lady Cicely passes out. There is a great stillness in the house. Mrs. Harding has watched Lady Cicely and Sir John in amazement. Sir John has sunk into a chair. She breaks out, "John, for God's sake what does it mean—this woman—speak—there is something awful, I must know."

"Yes, you must know. It is fate. Margaret, you do not know all. Two years ago I married——"

"But this woman, this woman——"

"She is—she was—my wife."

. . . .

And at this moment Harding breaks into the room. "Cicely, Cicely, I was too late——" He sees the others. "Mother," he says in agony, "and you——" He looks about. "Where is she? What is happening? I must know——"

Sir John, as if following a mechanical impulse, has handed Harding the letter. He tears it open and reads:

"Dearest, I am going away, to die. It cannot be long now. The doctor told me to-day. That was why I couldn't speak or explain it to you and was so strange at supper. But I am glad now. Good-by."

Harding turns upon Sir John with the snarl of a wolf. "What have you done? Why have you driven her away? What right had you to her, you devil? I loved her—She was mine——"

He had seized a pointed knife from the supper table. His shoulders are crouched—he is about to spring on Sir John. Mrs. Harding has thrown herself between them.

"Jack, Jack, you mustn't strike."

"Out of the way, I say, I'll——"

"Jack, Jack, you mustn't strike. Can't you understand? Don't you see—what it is. . . ."

"What do you mean—stand back from me."

"Jack he—is—your—father."

The knife clatters to the floor. "My God!"

And then the curtain falls—and there's a burst of applause and, in accordance with all the best traditions of the stage, one moment later, Lady Cicely and Mr. Harding and Sir John and Mrs. Harding are all bowing and smiling like anything, and even the little French maid sneaks on in a corner of the stage and simpers.

Then the orchestra plays and the leopards sneak out and the people in the boxes are all talking gayly to show that they're not the least affected. And everybody is wondering how it will come out, or rather how it can *possibly* come out at all, because some of them explain that it's all wrong, and just as they are making it clear that there shouldn't be any third act, the curtain goes up and it's——

Act III. Three Months Later

THE curtain rises on a drawing-room in Mrs. Harding's house in London. Mrs. Harding is sitting at a table. She is sorting out parcels. There is a great air of quiet about the scene. The third act of a problem play always has to be very quiet. It is like a punctured football with the wind going out of it. The play has to just poof itself out noiselessly.

For instance, this is the way it is done.

Does Mrs. Harding start to talk about Lady Cicely and Jack, and Paris? Not a bit. She is simply looking over the parcels and writing names and talking to herself so that the audience can get the names

"For the Orphans' Home—poor little things. For the Foundlings' Protection Society. For the Lost Infants' Preservation League" (a deep sigh)—"poor, poor children."

Now what is all this about? What has this

to do with the play? Why, don't you see that it is the symbol of philanthropy, of gentleness, of melancholy sadness? The storm is over and there is nothing in Mrs. Harding's heart but pity. Don't you see that she is dressed in deeper black than ever, and do you notice that look on her face—that third-act air—that resignation?

Don't you see that the play is really all over? They're just letting the wind out of it.

A man announces "Sir John Trevor."

Sir John steps in. Mrs. Harding goes to meet him with both hands out.

"My dear, dear friend," she says in rich, sad tones.

Sir John is all in black. He is much aged, but very firm and very quiet. You can feel that he's been spending the morning with the committee of the Homeless Newsboys' League or among the Directorate of the Lost Waifs' Encouragement Association. In fact he begins to talk of these things at once. The people who are not used to third acts are wondering what it is all about. The real playgoers know that this is *atmosphere.*

Then presently——

"Tea?" says Mrs. Harding, "shall I ring?"

"Pray do," says Sir John. He seats himself with great weariness. The full melancholy of the third act is on him. The tea which has been made for three acts is brought in. They drink it and it begins to go to their heads. The "atmosphere" clears off just a little.

"You have news, I know," says Mrs. Harding, "you have seen him?"

"I have seen him."

"And he is gone?"

"Yes, he has sailed," says Sir John. "He went on board last night, only a few hours after my return to London. I saw him off. Poor Jack. Gatherson has been most kind. They will take him into the embassy at Lima. There, please God, he can begin life again. The Peruvian Ambassador has promised to do all in his power."

Sir John sighs deeply and is silent. This to

let the fact soak into the audience that Jack has gone to Peru. Any reasonable person would have known it. Where else could he go to?

"He will do well in Peru," says Mrs. Harding. She is imitating a woman being very brave.

"Yes, I trust so," says Sir John. There is silence again. In fact the whole third act is diluted with thirty per cent. of silence. Presently Mrs. Harding speaks again in a low tone.

"You have other news, I know."

"I have other news."

"Of her?"

"Yes. I have been to Switzerland. I have seen the curé—a good man. He has told me all there is to tell. I found him at the hospice, busy with his *œuvre de bienfaisance.* He led me to her grave."

Sir John is bowed in deep silence.

Lady Cicely dead! Everybody in the theater gasps. Dead! But what an unfair way to kill her! To face an open death on the stage in fair hand to hand acting is one thing, but this new system of dragging off the characters to Switzerland between the acts, and then returning and saying that they are dead is quite another.

Presently Mrs. Harding speaks, very softly. "And you? You will take up your work here again?"

"No; I am going away."

"Going?"

"Yes, far away. I am going to Kafoonistan."

Mrs. Harding looks at him in pain. "To Kafoonistan?"

"Yes. To Kafoonistan. There's work there for me to do."

. . . .

There is silence again. Then Sir John speaks. "And you? You will settle down here in London?"

"No. I am going away."

"Going away?"

"Yes, back to Balla Walla. I want to be

alone. I want to forget. I want to think. I want to try to realize."

"You are going alone?"

"Yes, quite alone. But I shall not feel alone when I get there. The Maharanee will receive me with open arms. And my life will be useful there. The women need me; I will teach them to read, to sew, to sing."

"Mrs. Harding—Margaret—you must not do this. You have sacrificed your life enough—you have the right to live——"

There is emotion in Sir John's tone. It is very rough on him to find his plan of going to Kafoonistan has been outdone by Mrs. Harding's going to Balla Walla. She shakes her head.

"No, no; my life is of no account now. But you, John, you are needed here, the country needs you. Men look to you to lead them."

Mrs. Harding would particularize if she could, but she can't just for the minute remember what it is Sir John can lead them to. Sir John shakes his head.

"No, no; my work lies there in Kafoonistan.

There is a man's work to be done there. The tribes are ignorant, uncivilized."

This dialogue goes on for some time. Mrs. Harding keeps shaking her head and saying that Sir John must not go to Kafoonistan, and Sir John says she must not go to Balla Walla. He protests that he wants to work and she claims that she wants to try to think clearly. But it is all a bluff. They are not going. Neither of them. And everybody knows it. Presently Mrs. Harding says:

"You will think of me sometimes?"

"I shall never forget you."

"I'm glad of that."

"Wherever I am, I shall think of you—out there in the deserts, or at night, alone there among the great silent hills with only the stars overhead, I shall think of you. Your face will guide me wherever I am."

He has taken her hand.

"And you," he says, "you will think of me sometimes in Balla Walla?"

"Yes, always. All day while I am with the Maharanee and her women, and at night, the great silent Indian night when all the palace is asleep and there is heard nothing but the sounds of the jungle, the cry of the hyena and the bray of the laughing jackass, I shall seem to hear your voice."

She is much moved. She rises, clenches her hands and then adds, "I have heard it so for five and twenty years."

He has moved to her.

"Margaret!"

"John!"

"I cannot let you go, your life lies here—with me—next my heart—I want your help, your love, here inside the beyond."

And as he speaks and takes her in his arms, the curtain sinks upon them, rises, falls, rises, and then sinks again asbestos and all, and the play is over. The lights are on, the audience rises in a body and puts on its wraps. All over the theater you can hear the words "perfectly rotten," "utterly untrue," and so on. The general judgment seems to be that it is a perfectly rotten play, but very strong.

They are saying this as they surge out in

great waves of furs and silks, with black crush hats floating on billows of white wraps among the foam of gossamer scarfs. Through it all is the squawk of the motor horn, the call of the taxi numbers and the inrush of the fresh night air.

But just inside the theater, in the office, is a man in a circus waistcoat adding up dollars with a blue pencil, and he knows that the play is all right.

He takes her in his arms.

FAMILIAR INCIDENTS

I.—With the Photographer

I WANT my photograph taken," I said. The photographer looked at me without enthusiasm. He was a drooping man in a gray suit, with the dim eye of a natural scientist. But there is no need to describe him. Everybody knows what a photographer is like.

"Sit there," he said, "and wait."

"I waited an hour. I read the *Ladies Companion* for 1912, the *Girls Magazine* for 1902 and the *Infants Journal* for 1888. I began to see that I had done an unwarrantable thing in breaking in on the privacy of this man's scientific pursuits with a face like mine.

After an hour the photographer opened the inner door.

"Come in," he said severely.

I went into the studio.

"Sit down," said the photographer.

I sat down in a beam of sunlight filtered

through a sheet of factory cotton hung against a frosted skylight.

The photographer rolled a machine into the middle of the room and crawled into it from behind.

He was only in it a second,—just time enough for one look at me,—and then he was out again, tearing at the cotton sheet and the window panes with a hooked stick, apparently frantic for light and air.

Then he crawled back into the machine again and drew a little black cloth over himself. This time he was very quiet in there. I knew that he was praying and I kept still.

When the photographer came out at last, he looked very grave and shook his head.

"The face is quite wrong," he said.

"I know," I answered quietly; "I have always known it."

He sighed.

"I think," he said, "the face would be better three-quarters full."

"I'm sure it would," I said enthusiastically, for I was glad to find that the man had such a human side to him. "So would yours. In fact," I continued, "how many faces one sees that are apparently hard, narrow, limited, but the minute you get them three-quarters full they get wide, large, almost boundless in——"

But the photographer had ceased to listen. He came over and took my head in his hands and twisted it sideways. I thought he meant to kiss me, and I closed my eyes.

But I was wrong.

He twisted my face as far as it would go and then stood looking at it.

He sighed again.

"I don't like the head," he said.

Then he went back to the machine and took another look.

"Open the mouth a little," he said.

I started to do so.

"Close it," he added quickly.

Then he looked again.

"The ears are *bad*," he said; "droop them a little more. Thank you. Now the eyes. Roll them in under the lids. Put the hands on the knees, please, and turn the face just a little upward. Yes, that's better. Now just expand the lungs! So! And hump the neck—that's it—and just contract the waist—ha!—and twist the hip up toward the elbow—now! I still don't quite like the face, it's just a trifle *too* full, but——"

I swung myself round on the stool.

"Stop," I said with emotion but, I think, with dignity. "This face is *my* face. It is not yours, it is mine. I've lived with it for forty years and I know its faults. I know it's out of drawing. I know it wasn't made for me, but it's *my* face, the only one I have—" I was conscious of a break in my voice but I went on—"such as it is, I've learned to love it. And this is my mouth, not yours. These ears are *mine,* and if your machine is too narrow—" Here I started to rise from the seat.

Snick!

The photographer had pulled a string. The photograph taken. I could see the machine still staggering from the shock.

"I think," said the photographer, pursing

his lips in a pleased smile, "that I caught the features just in a moment of animation."

"So!" I said bitingly,—"features, eh? You didn't think I could animate them, I suppose? But let me see the picture."

"Oh, there's nothing to see yet," he said, "I have to develop the negative first. Come back on Saturday and I'll let you see a proof of it."

On Saturday I went back.

The photographer beckoned me in. I thought he seemed quieter and graver than before. I think, too, there was a certain pride in his manner.

He unfolded the proof of a large photograph, and we both looked at it in silence.

"Is it me?" I asked.

"Yes," he said quietly, "it is you," and we went on looking at it.

"The eyes," I said hesitatingly, "don't look very much like mine."

"Oh, no," he answered, "I've retouched them. They come out splendidly, don't they?"

"Fine," I said, "but surely my eyebrows are not like that?"

"No," said the photographer, with a momentary glance at my face, "the eyebrows are removed. We have a process now—the Delphide—for putting in new ones. You'll notice here where we've applied it to carry the hair away from the brow. I don't like the hair low on the skull."

"Oh, you don't, don't you?" I said.

"No," he went on, "I don't care for it. I like to get the hair clear back to the superficies and make out a new brow line."

"What about the mouth?" I said with a bitterness that was lost on the photographer; "is that mine?"

"It's adjusted a little," he said, "yours is too low. I found I couldn't use it."

"The ears, though," I said, "strike me as a good likeness; they're just like mine."

"Yes," said the photographer thoughtfully, "that's so; but I can fix that all right in the print. We have a process now—the Sulphide

"Is it me?"

—for removing the ears entirely. I'll see if——"

"Listen!" I interrupted, drawing myself up and animating my features to their full extent and speaking with a withering scorn that should have blasted the man on the spot. "Listen! I came here for a photograph—a picture—something which (mad though it seems) would have looked like me. I wanted something that would depict my face as Heaven gave it to me, humble though the gift may have been. I wanted something that my friends might keep after my death, to reconcile them to my loss. It seems that I was mistaken. What I wanted is no longer done. Go on, then, with your brutal work. Take your negative, or whatever it is you call it,—dip it in sulphide, bromide, oxide, cowhide,—anything you like,—remove the eyes, correct the mouth, adjust the face, restore the lips, reanimate the necktie and reconstruct the waistcoat. Coat it with an inch of gloss, shade it, emboss it, gild it, till even you acknowledge that it is finished.

Then when you have done all that—keep it for yourself and your friends. They may value it. To me it is but a worthless bauble."

I broke into tears and left.

II.—*The Dentist and the Gas*

"I THINK," said the dentist, stepping outside again, "I'd better give you gas."

Then he moved aside and hummed an air from a light opera while he mixed up cement:

I sat up in my shroud.

"Gas!" I said.

"Yes," he repeated, "gas, or else ether or a sulphuric anesthetic, or else beat you into insensibility with a club, or give you three thousand bolts of electricity."

These may not have been his exact words. But they convey the feeling of them very nicely.

I could see the light of primitive criminality shining behind the man's spectacles.

And to think that this was *my* fault—the result of my own reckless neglect. I had grown so used to sitting back dozing in my shroud in the dentist's chair, listening to the twittering of the birds outside, my eyes closed in the sweet half sleep of perfect security, that the old apprehensiveness and mental agony had practically all gone.

He didn't hurt me, and I knew it.

I had grown—I know it sounds mad—almost to like him.

For a time I had kept up the appearance of being hurt every few minutes, just as a precaution. Then even that had ceased and I had dropped into vainglorious apathy.

It was this, of course, which had infuriated the dentist. He meant to reassert his power. He knew that nothing but gas could rouse me out of my lethargy and he meant to apply it—either gas or some other powerful pain stimulant.

So, as soon as he said "*gas*," my senses were alert in a moment.

"When are you going to do it?" I said in horror.

"Right now, if you like," he answered.

His eyes were glittering with what the Germans call *Blutlust*. All dentists have it.

I could see that if I took my eye off him for a moment he might spring at me, gas in hand, and throttle me.

"No, not now, I can't stay now," I said, "I have an appointment, a whole lot of appointments, urgent ones, the most urgent I ever had." I was unfastening my shroud as I spoke.

"Well, then, to-morrow," said the dentist.

"No," I said, "to-morrow is Saturday. And Saturday is a day when I simply can't take gas. If I take gas, even the least bit of gas on a Saturday, I find it's misunderstood——"

"Monday then."

"Monday, I'm afraid, won't do. It's a bad day for me—worse than I can explain."

"Tuesday?" said the dentist.

"Not Tuesday," I answered. "Tuesday is the worst day of all. On Tuesday my church society meets, and I *must* go to it."

I hadn't been near it, in reality, for three years, but suddenly I felt a longing to attend it.

"On Wednesday," I went on, speaking hurriedly and wildly, "I have another appointment, a swimming club, and on Thursday two appointments, a choral society and a funeral. On Friday I have another funeral. Saturday is market day. Sunday is washing day. Monday is drying day——"

"Hold on," said the dentist, speaking very firmly. "You come to-morrow morning: I'll write the engagement for ten o'clock."

I think it must have been hypnotism.

Before I knew it, I had said "Yes."

I went out.

On the street I met a man I knew.

"Have you ever taken gas from a dentist?" I asked.

"Oh, yes," he said; "it's nothing."

Soon after I met another man.

"Have you ever taken gas?" I asked.

"Oh, certainly," he answered, "it's nothing, nothing at all."

Altogether I asked about fifty people that day about gas, and they all said that it was absolutely nothing. When I said that I was to take it to-morrow, they showed no concern whatever. I looked in their faces for traces of anxiety. There weren't any. They all said that it wouldn't hurt me, that it was nothing.

So then I was glad because I knew that gas was nothing.

It began to seem hardly worth while to keep the appointment. Why go all the way downtown for such a mere nothing?

But I did go.

I kept the appointment.

What followed was such an absolute nothing that I shouldn't bother to relate it except for the sake of my friends.

The dentist was there with two assistants. All three had white coats on, as rigid as naval uniforms.

I forget whether they carried revolvers.

Nothing could exceed their quiet courage. Let me pay them that tribute.

I was laid out in my shroud in a long chair and tied down to it (I think I was tied down; perhaps I was fastened with nails). This part of it was a mere nothing. It simply felt like being tied down by three strong men armed with pinchers.

After that a gas tank and a pump were placed beside me and a set of rubber tubes fastened tight over my mouth and nose. Even those who have never taken gas can realize how ridiculously simple this is.

Then they began pumping in gas. The sensation of this part of it I cannot, unfortunately, recall. It happened that just as they began to administer the gas, I fell asleep. I don't quite know why. Perhaps I was overtired. Perhaps it was the simple home charm of the surroundings, the soft drowsy hum of the gas pump, the twittering of the dentists in the trees—did I say the trees? No; of course they weren't in the trees—imagine dentists in the trees—ha! ha! Here, take off this gaspipe from my face till I laugh—really I just want to laugh—only to laugh——

Well,—that's what it felt like.

Meanwhile they were operating.

Of course I didn't *feel* it. All I felt was that someone dealt me a powerful blow in the face with a sledgehammer. After that some-

I did go...I kept the appointment.

body took a pickax and cracked in my jaw with it. That was all.

It was a mere nothing. I felt at the time that a man who objects to a few taps on the face with a pickax is overcritical.

I didn't happen to wake up till they had practically finished. So I really missed the whole thing.

The assistants had gone, and the dentist was mixing up cement and humming airs from light opera just like old times. It made the world seem a bright place.

I went home with no teeth. I only meant them to remove one, but I realized that they had taken them all out. Still it didn't matter.

Not long after I received my bill. I was astounded at the nerve of it! For administering gas, debtor, so much; for removing teeth, debtor, so much;—and so on.

In return I sent in my bill:

DR. WILLIAM JAWS

DEBTOR

To mental agony................	$50.00
To gross lies in regard to the nothingness of gas.............	100.00
To putting me under gas........	50.00
To having fun with me under gas.	100.00
To Brilliant Ideas, occurred to me under gas and lost..........	100.00
Grand Total	$400.00

My bill has been contested and is in the hands of a solicitor. The matter will prove, I understand, a test case and will go to the final courts. If the judges have toothache during the trial, I shall win.

III.—My Lost Opportunities

THE other day I took a walk with a real estate man. Out in the suburbs he leaned over the wooden fence of an empty lot and waved his hand at it.

"There's a lot," he said, "that we sold last week for half a million dollars."

"Did you really!" I exclaimed.

"Yes," he said, "and do you know that twenty-five years ago you could have picked that up for fifty thousand!"

"What," I said, "do you mean to say that I could have had all that beautiful grass and those mullin stalks for fifty thousand dollars?"

"I do."

"You mean that when I was a student at college, feeding on four dollars a week, this opportunity was knocking at the door and I missed it?"

I turned my head away in bitterness as I

thought of my own folly. Why had I never happened to walk out this way with fifty thousand dollars in my pocket and buy all this beautiful mud?

The real estate man smiled complacently at my grief.

"I can show you more than that," he said. "Do you see that big stretch of empty ground out there past that last fence?"

"Yes, yes," I said excitedly, "the land with the beautiful tar-paper shack and the withered cedar tree,—the one withered cedar tree,—standing in its lonely isolation and seeming to beckon——"

"Say," he said, "was you ever in the real estate business yourself?"

"No," I answered, "but I have a poetic mind, and I begin to see the poetry, the majesty, of real estate."

"Oh, is that it," he answered. "Well, that land out there,—it's an acre and a half,—was sold yesterday for three million dollars!!"

"For what!"

"For three million dollars, cold."

"Not COLD!" I said, "don't tell me it was cold."

"Yes," went on the real estate man, "and only three years ago you could have come out here and had it for a song!"

"For a song!" I repeated.

Just think of it! And I had missed it! With a voice like mine. If I had known what I know now, I would have come out to that land and sung to it all night. I never knew in the days when I was content with fifteen dollars a week what a hidden gift my voice was. I should have taken up land-singing and made a fortune out of it.

The thought of it saddened me all the way home: and the talk of the real estate man as he went made me feel still worse.

He showed me a church that I could have bought for a hundred thousand and sold now at half a million for a motor garage. If I had started buying churches instead of working on a newspaper, I'd have been rich to-day.

There was a skating rink I could have bought, and a theatre and a fruit store, a beautiful little one-story wooden fruit store, right on a corner, with the darlingest Italian in it that you ever saw. There was the cutest little pet of a cow-stable that I could have turned into an apartment store at a profit of a million,—at the time when I was studying Greek and forgetting it. Oh! the wasted opportunities of life!

And that evening when I got back to the club and talked about it at dinner to my business friends, I found that I had only heard a small part of it.

Real estate! That's nothing! Why they told me that fifteen years ago I could have had all sorts of things,—trunk line railways, sugar refineries, silver mines,—any of them for a song. When I heard it I was half glad I hadn't sung for the land. They told me that there was a time when I could have bought out the Federal Steel Co. for twenty million dollars! And I let it go.

The whole Canadian Pacific Railway, they said, was thrown on the market for fifty millions. I left it there writhing, and didn't pick

He showed me a church that I could have bought for a hundred thousand.

it up. Sheer lack of confidence! I see now why these men get rich. It's their fine, glorious confidence, that enables them to write out a cheque for fifty million dollars and think nothing of it.

If I wrote a cheque like that, I'd be afraid of going to Sing Sing. But they aren't, and so they get what they deserve.

Forty-five years ago,—a man at the club told me this with almost a sob in his voice,—either Rockefeller or Carnegie could have been bought clean up for a thousand dollars!

Think of it!

Why didn't my father buy them for me, as pets, for my birthday and let me keep them till I grew up?

If I had my life over again, no school or education for me! Not with all this beautiful mud and these tar-paper shacks and corner lot fruit stores lying round! I'd buy out the whole United States and take a chance, a sporting chance, on the rise in values.

IV.—My Unknown Friend

HE STEPPED into the smoking compartment of the Pullman, where I was sitting alone.

He had on a long fur-lined coat, and he carried a fifty-dollar suit case that he put down on the seat.

Then he saw me.

"Well! well!" he said, and recognition broke out all over his face like morning sunlight.

"Well! well!" I repeated.

"By Jove!" he said, shaking hands vigorously, "who would have thought of seeing you?"

"Who, indeed," I thought to myself.

He looked at me more closely.

"You haven't changed a bit," he said.

"Neither have you," said I heartily.

"You may be a *little* stouter," he went on critically.

"Yes," I said, "a little; but you're stouter yourself."

This of course would help to explain away any undue stoutness on my part.

"No," I continued boldly and firmly, "you look just about the same as ever."

And all the time I was wondering who he was. I didn't know him from Adam; I couldn't recall him a bit. I don't mean that my memory is weak. On the contrary, it is singularly tenacious. True, I find it very hard to remember people's *names*; very often, too, it is hard for me to recall a *face,* and frequently I fail to recall a person's appearance, and of course clothes are a thing one doesn't notice. But apart from these details I never forget anybody, and I am proud of it. But when it does happen that a name or face escapes me I never lose my presence of mind. I know just how to deal with the situation. It only needs coolness and intellect, and it all comes right.

My friend sat down.

"It's a long time since we met," he said.

"A long time," I repeated with something of a note of sadness. I wanted him to feel that I, too, had suffered from it.

"But it has gone very quickly."

"Like a flash," I assented cheerfully.

"Strange," he said, "how life goes on and we lose track of people, and things alter. I often think about it. I sometimes wonder," he continued, "where all the old gang are gone to."

"So do I," I said. In fact I was wondering about it at the very moment. I always find in circumstances like these that a man begins sooner or later to talk of the "old gang" or "the boys" or "the crowd." That's where the opportunity comes in to gather who he is.

"Do you ever go back to the old place?" he asked.

"Never," I said, firmly and flatly. This had to be absolute. I felt that once and for all the "old place" must be ruled out of the discussion till I could discover where it was.

"No," he went on, "I suppose you'd hardly care to."

"Not now," I said very gently.

"I understand. I beg your pardon," he said, and there was silence for a few moments.

So far I had scored the first point. There was evidently an old place somewhere to which I would hardly care to go. That was something to build on.

Presently he began again.

"Yes," he said, "I sometimes meet some of the old boys and they begin to talk of you and wonder what you're doing."

"Poor things," I thought, but I didn't say it.

I knew it was time now to make a bold stroke; so I used the method that I always employ. I struck in with great animation.

"Say!" I said, "where's Billy? Do you ever hear anything of Billy now?"

This is really a very safe line. Every old gang has a Billy in it.

"Yes," said my friend, "sure—Billy is ranching out in Montana. I saw him in Chicago last spring,—weighed about two hundred pounds,—you wouldn't know him."

"No, I certainly wouldn't," I murmured to myself.

"And where's Pete?" I said. This was safe ground. There is always a Pete.

"You mean Billy's brother," he said.

"Yes, yes, Billy's brother Pete. I often think of him."

"Oh," answered the unknown man, "old Pete's quite changed,—settled down altogether." Here he began to chuckle, "Why, Pete's married!"

I started to laugh, too. Under these circumstances it is always supposed to be very funny if a man has got married. The notion of old Peter (whoever he is) being married is presumed to be simply killing. I kept on chuckling away quietly at the mere idea of it. I was hoping that I might manage to keep on laughing till the train stopped. I had only fifty miles more to go. It's not hard to laugh for fifty miles if you know how.

But my friend wouldn't be content with it.

"I often meant to write to you," he said,

his voice falling to a confidential tone, "especially when I heard of your loss."

I remained quiet. What had I lost? Was it money? And if so, how much? And why had I lost it? I wondered if it had ruined me or only partly ruined me.

"One can never get over a loss like that," he continued solemnly.

Evidently I was plumb ruined. But I said nothing and remained under cover, waiting to draw his fire.

"Yes," the man went on, "death is always sad."

Death! Oh, that was it, was it? I almost hiccoughed with joy. That was easy. Handling a case of death in these conversations is simplicity itself. One has only to sit quiet and wait to find out who is dead.

"Yes," I murmured, "very sad. But it has its other side, too."

"Very true, especially, of course, at that age."

"As you say at that age, and after such a life."

"Strong and bright to the last I suppose," he continued, very sympathetically.

"Yes," I said, falling on sure ground, "able to sit up in bed and smoke within a few days of the end."

"What," he said, perplexed, "did your grandmother——"

My grandmother! That was it, was it?

"Pardon *me,*" I said provoked at my own stupidity; "when I say *smoked,* I mean able to sit up and be smoked to, a habit she had,—being read to, and being smoked to,—only thing that seemed to compose her——"

As I said this I could hear the rattle and clatter of the train running past the semaphores and switch points and slacking to a stop.

My friend looked quickly out of the window.

His face was agitated.

"Great heavens!" he said, "that's the junction. I've missed my stop. I should have got out at the last station. Say, porter," he called out into the alleyway, "how long do we stop here?"

"Just two minutes, sah," called a voice back. "She's late now, she's makin' up tahm!"

My friend had hopped up now and had pulled out a bunch of keys and was fumbling at the lock of the suit case.

"I'll have to wire back or something," he gasped. "Confound this lock—my money's in the suit case."

My one fear now was that he would fail to get off.

"Here," I said, pulling some money out of my pocket, "don't bother with the lock. Here's money."

"Thanks," he said grabbing the roll of money out of my hand,—in his excitement he took all that I had.—"I'll just have time."

He sprang from the train. I saw him through the window, moving toward the waiting-room. He didn't seem going very fast.

I waited.

The porters were calling, "All abawd! All abawd." There was the clang of a bell, a hiss of steam, and in a second the train was off.

"Idiot," I thought, "he's missed it;" and there was his fifty-dollar suit case lying on the seat.

I waited, looking out of the window and wondering who the man was, anyway.

Then presently I heard the porter's voice again. He evidently was guiding someone through the car.

"Ah looked all through the kyar for it, sah," he was saying.

"I left it in the seat in the car there behind my wife," said the angry voice of a stranger, a well-dressed man who put his head into the door of the compartment.

Then his face, too, beamed all at once with recognition. But it was not for me. It was for the fifty-dollar valise.

"Ah, there it is," he cried, seizing it and carrying it off.

I sank back in dismay. The "old gang!" Pete's marriage! My grandmother's death! Great heavens! And my money! I saw it all;

the other man was "making talk," too, and making it with a purpose.

Stung!

And next time that I fall into talk with a casual stranger in a car, I shall not try to be quite so extraordinarily clever.

V.—Under the Barber's Knife

WAS you to the Arena the other night?" said the barber, leaning over me and speaking in his confidential whisper.

"Yes," I said, "I was there."

He saw from this that I could still speak. So he laid another thick wet towel over my face before he spoke again.

"What did you think of the game," he asked.

But he had miscalculated. I could still make a faint sound through the wet towels. He laid three or four more very thick ones over my face and stood with his five finger tips pressed against my face for support. A thick steam rose about me. Through it I could hear the barber's voice and the flick-flack of the razor as he stropped it.

"Yes, sir," he went on in his quiet professional tone, punctuated with the noise of the razor, "I knowed from the start them boys

I shall not try to be quite so extraordinarily clever.

was sure to win,"—flick-flack-flick-flack,—"as soon as I seen the ice that night and seen the get-away them boys made I knowed it,"—flick-flack,—"and just as soon as Jimmy got aholt of the puck——"

This was more than the barber at the next chair could stand.

"Him get de puck," he cried, giving an angry dash with a full brush of soap into the face of the man under him,—"him get ut-dat stiff—why, boys," he said, and he turned appealingly to the eight barbers, who all rested their elbows on the customers' faces while they listened to the rising altercation; even the manicure girl, thrilled to attention, clasped tight the lumpy hand of her client in her white digits and remained motionless,—"why boys, dat feller can't no more play hockey than——"

"See here," said the barber, suddenly and angrily, striking his fist emphatically on the towels that covered my face. "I'll bet you five dollars to one Jimmy can skate rings round any two men in the league."

"Him skate," sneered the other squirting a

jet of blinding steam in the face of the client he was treating, "he ain't got no more go in him than dat rag,"—and he slapped a wet towel across his client's face.

All the barbers were excited now. There was a babel of talk from behind each of the eight chairs. "He can't skate;" "He can skate;" "I'll bet you ten."

Already they were losing their tempers, slapping their customers with wet towels and jabbing great brushfuls of soap into their mouths. My barber was leaning over my face with his whole body. In another minute one or the other of them would have been sufficiently provoked to have dealt his customer a blow behind the ear.

Then suddenly there was a hush.

"The boss," said one.

In another minute I could realize, though I couldn't see it, that a majestic figure in a white coat was moving down the line. All was still again except the quiet hum of the mechanical shampoo brush and the soft burble of running water.

The barber began removing the wet towels from my face one by one. He peeled them off with the professional neatness of an Egyptologist unwrapping a mummy. When he reached my face he looked searchingly at it. There was suspicion in his eye.

"Been out of town?" he questioned.

"Yes," I admitted.

"Who's been doing your work?" he asked. This question, from a barber, has no reference to one's daily occupation. It means "who has been shaving you."

I knew it was best to own up. I'd been in the wrong, and I meant to acknowledge it with perfect frankness.

"I've been shaving myself," I said.

My barber stood back from me in contempt. There was a distinct sensation all down the line of barbers. One of them threw a wet rag in a corner with a thud, and another sent a sudden squirt from an atomizer into his customer's eyes as a mark of disgust.

My barber continued to look at me narrowly.

"What razor do you use?" he said.

"A safety razor," I answered.

The barber had begun to dash soap over my face; but he stopped—aghast at what I had said.

A safety razor to a barber is like a red rag to a bull.

"If it was me," he went on, beating lather into me as he spoke, "I wouldn't let one of them things near my face: No, sir: There ain't no safety in them. They tear the hide clean off you—just rake the hair right out by the follicles," as he said this he was illustrating his meaning with jabs of his razor,—"them things just cut a man's face all to pieces," he jabbed a stick of alum against an open cut that he had made,—"And as for cleanliness, for sanitation, for this here hygiene and for germs, I wouldn't have them round me for a fortune."

I said nothing. I knew I had deserved it, and I kept quiet.

The barber gradually subsided. Under other circumstances he would have told me

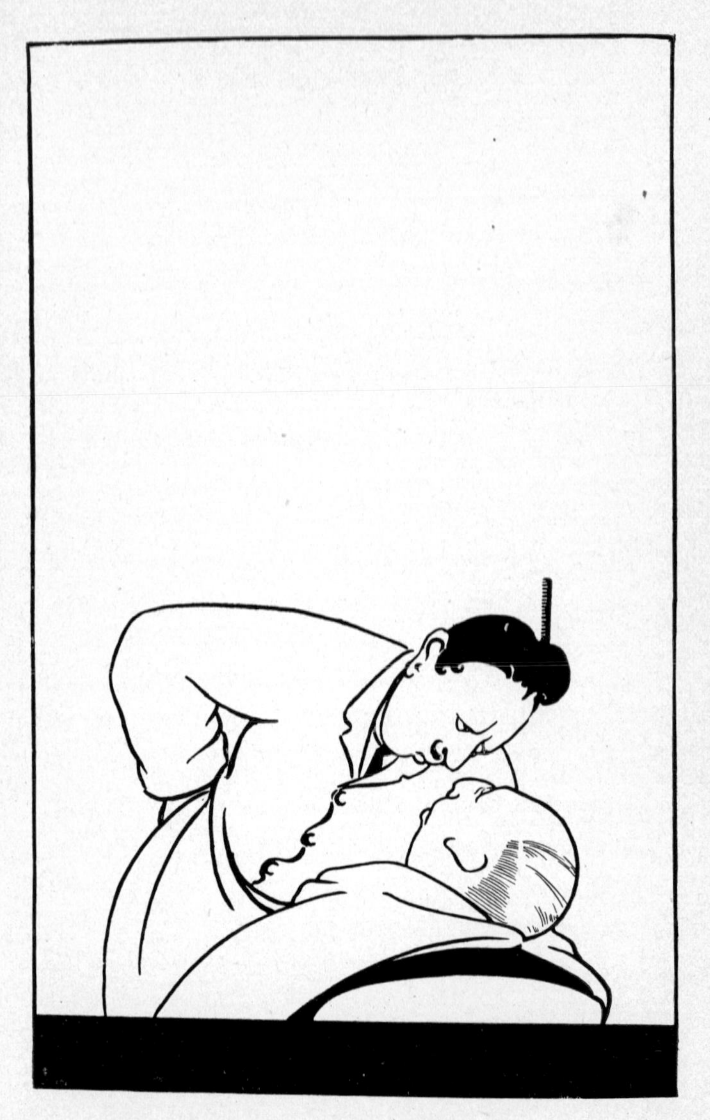

When he reached my face he looked searchingly at it.

something of the spring training of the baseball clubs, or the last items from the Jacksonville track, or any of those things which a cultivated man loves to hear discussed between breakfast and business. But I was not worth it. As he neared the end of the shaving he spoke again, this time in a confidential, almost yearning, tone.

"Massage?" he said.

"No thank you."

"Shampoo the scalp?" he whispered.

"No thanks."

"Singe the hair?" he coaxed.

"No thanks."

The barber made one more effort.

"Say," he said in my ear, as a thing concerning himself and me alone, "your hair's pretty well all falling out. You'd better let me just shampoo up the scalp a bit and stop up them follicles or pretty soon you won't—"

"No, thank you," I said, "not to-day."

This was all the barber could stand. He saw that I was just one of those miserable dead-beats who come to a barber shop merely for a shave, and who carry away the scalp and the follicles and all the barber's perquisites as if they belonged to them.

In a second he had me thrown out of the chair.

"Next," he shouted.

As I passed down the line of the barbers, I could see contempt in every eye while they turned on the full clatter of their revolving shampoo brushes and drowned the noise of my miserable exit in the roar of machinery.

PARISIAN PASTIMES

I.—The Advantages of a Polite Education

"TAKE it from me," said my friend from Kansas, leaning back in his seat at the Taverne Royale and holding his cigar in his two fingers—"don't talk no French here in Paris. They don't expect it, and they don't seem to understand it."

This man from Kansas, mind you, had a right to speak. He *knew* French. He had learned French—he told me so himself—*good* French, at the Fayetteville Classical Academy. Later on he had had the natural method "off" a man from New Orleans. It had cost him "fifty cents a throw." All this I have on his own word. But in France something seemed to go wrong with his French.

"No," he said reflectively, "I guess what most of them speak here is a sort of patois."

When he said it was a patois, I knew just what he meant. It was equivalent to saying that he couldn't understand it.

I had seen him strike patois before. There had been a French steward on the steamer coming over, and the man from Kansas, after a couple of attempts, had said it was no use talking French to that man. He spoke a hopeless patois. There were half a dozen cabin passengers, too, returning to their homes in France. But we soon found from listening to their conversation on deck that what they were speaking was not French but some sort of patois.

It was the same thing coming through Normandy. Patois, everywhere, not a word of French—not a single sentence of the real language, in the way they had it at Fayetteville. We stopped off a day at Rouen to look at the cathedral. A sort of abbot showed us round. Would you believe it, that man spoke patois, straight patois—the very worst kind, and fast. The man from Kansas had spotted it at once.

He hadn't listened to more than ten sentences before he recognized it. "Patois," he said.

Of course, it's fine to be able to detect patois like this. It's impressive. The mere fact that you know the word patois shows that you must be mighty well educated.

Here in Paris it was the same way. Everybody that the man from Kansas tried—waiters, hotel clerks, shop people—all spoke patois. An educated person couldn't follow it.

On the whole, I think the advice of the man from Kansas is good. When you come to Paris, leave French behind. You don't need it, and they don't expect it of you.

In any case, you soon learn from experience not to use it.

If you try to, this is what happens. You summon a waiter to you and you say to him very slowly, syllable by syllable, so as to give him every chance in case he's not an educated man:

"Bringez moi de la soupe, de la fish, de la roast pork et de la fromage."

And he answers:

"Yes, sir, roast pork, sir, and a little bacon on the side?"

That waiter was raised in Illinois.

Or suppose you stop a man on the street and you say to him:

"Musshoo, s'il vous plait, which is la direction pour aller à le Palais Royal?"

And he answers:

"Well, I tell you, I'm something of a stranger here myself, but I guess it's straight down there a piece."

Now it's no use speculating whether that man comes from Dordogne Inférieure or from Auvergne-sur-les-Puits because he doesn't.

On the other hand, you may strike a real Frenchman—there are some even in Paris. I met one the other day in trying to find my way about, and I asked him:

"Musshoo, s'il vous plait, which is la direction pour aller à Thomas Cook & Son?"

"B'n'm'ss'ulvla'n'fsse'n'sse'pas!"

I said: "Thank you so much! I had half suspected it myself." But I didn't really know what he meant.

So I have come to make it a rule never to use French unless driven to it. Thus, for example, I had a tremendous linguistic struggle in a French tailors shop.

There was a sign in the window to the effect that "completes" might be had "for a hundred." It seemed a chance not to be missed. Moreover, the same sign said that English and German were spoken.

So I went in. True to my usual principle of ignoring the French language, I said to the head man:

"You speak English?"

He shrugged his shoulders, spread out his hands and looked at the clock on the wall.

"Presently," he said.

"Oh," I said, "you'll speak it presently. That's splendid. But why not speak it right away?"

The tailor again looked at the clock with a despairing shrug.

"At twelve o'clock," he said.

"Come now," I said, "be fair about this.

I don't want to wait an hour and a half for you to begin to talk. Let's get at it right now."

But he was obdurate. He merely shook his head and repeated:

"Speak English at twelve o'clock."

Judging that he must be under a vow of abstinence during the morning, I tried another idea.

"Allemand?" I asked, "German, Deutsch, eh! speak that?"

Again the French tailor shook his head, this time with great decision.

"Not till four o'clock," he said.

This was evidently final. He might be lax enough to talk English at noon, but he refused point-blank to talk German till he had his full strength.

I was just wondering whether there wasn't some common sense in this after all, when the solution of it struck me.

"Ah!" I said, speaking in French, "très bong! there is somebody who comes at twelve, quelqu'un qui vient à midi, who can talk English."

The tailor shrugged his shoulders.

"Precisément," said the tailor, wreathed in smiles and waving his tape coquettishly about his neck.

"You flirt!" I said, "but let's get to business. I want a suit, un soot, un complete, complet, comprenez-vous, veston, gilet, une pair de panteloon—everything—do you get it?"

The tailor was now all animation.

"Ah, certainement," he said, "monsieur desires a fantasy, une fantaisie, is it not?"

A fantasy! Good heavens!

The man had evidently got the idea from my naming so many things that I wanted a suit for a fancy dress carnival.

"Fantasy nothing!" I said—"pas de fantaisie! un soot anglais"—here an idea struck me and I tapped myself on the chest—"like this," I said, "comme ceci."

"Bon," said the tailor, now perfectly satisfied, "une fantaisie comme porte monsieur."

Here I got mad.

"Blast you," I said, "this is not a fantaisie. Do you take me for a dragon-fly, or what?

Now come, let's get this fantaisie business cleared up. This is what I want"—and here I put my hand on a roll of very quiet grey cloth on the counter.

"Très bien," said the tailor, "une fantaisie."

I stared at him.

"Is *that* a fantaisie?"

"Certainement, monsieur."

"Now," I said, "let's go into it further," and I touched another piece of plain pepper and salt stuff of the kind that is called in the simple and refined language of my own country, gents' panting.

"This?"

"Une fantaisie," said the French tailor.

"Well," I said, "you've got more imagination than I have."

Then I touched a piece of purple blue that would have been almost too loud for a Carolina nigger.

"Is this a fantaisie?"

The tailor shrugged his shoulders.

"Ah, non," he said in deprecating tones.

"Tell me," I said, speaking in French, "just exactly what it is you call a fantasy."

The tailor burst into a perfect paroxysm of French, gesticulating and waving his tape as he put the sentences over the plate one after another. It was fast pitching, but I took them every one, and I got him.

What he meant was that any single colour or combination of single colours—for instance, a pair of sky blue breeches with pink insertion behind—is not regarded by a French tailor as a fantaisie or fancy. But any mingled colour, such as the ordinary drab grey of the business man is a fantaisie of the daintiest kind. To the eye of a Parisian tailor, a Quakers' meeting is a glittering panorama of fantaisies, whereas a negro ball at midnight in a yellow room with a band in scarlet, is a plain, simple scene.

I thanked him. Then I said:

"Measure me, mesurez-moi, passez le tape line autour de moi."

He did it.

I don't know what it is they measure you

in, whether in centimètres or cubic feet or what it is. But the effect is appalling.

The tailor runs his tape round your neck and calls "sixty!" Then he puts it round the lower part of the back—at the major circumference, you understand,—and shouts, "a hundred and fifty!"

It sounded a record breaker. I felt that there should have been a burst of applause. But, to tell the truth, I have friends—quiet sedentary men in the professoriate—who would easily hit up four or five hundred on the same scale.

Then came the last item.

"Now," I said, "when will this 'complete' be ready?"

"Ah, monsieur," said the tailor, with winsome softness, "we are very busy, crushed, écrasés with commands! Give us time, don't hurry us!"

"Well," I said, "how long do you want?"

"Ah, monsieur," he pleaded, "give us four days!"

I never moved an eyelash.

"What!" I said indignantly, "four days! Monstrous! Let me have this whole complete fantasy in one day or I won't buy it."

"Ah, monsieur, three days?"

"No," I said, "make it two days."

"Two days and a half, monsieur."

"Two days and a quarter," I said; "give it me the day after to-morrow at three o'clock in the morning."

"Ah, monsieur, ten o'clock."

"Make it ten minutes to ten and it's a go," I said.

"Bon," said the tailor.

He kept his word. I am wearing the fantaisie as I write. For a fantaisie, it is fairly quiet, except that it has three pockets on each side outside, and a rolled back collar suitable for the throat of an opera singer, and as many buttons as a harem skirt. Beyond that, it's a first-class, steady, reliable, quiet, religious fantaisie, such as any retired French ballet master might be proud to wear.

II.—The Joys of Philanthropy

"GOOD-MORNING," said the valet de chambre, as I stepped from my room.

"Good-morning," I answered. "Pray accept twenty-five centimes."

"Good-morning, sir," said the maître d'hôtel, as I passed down the corridor, "a lovely morning, sir."

"So lovely," I replied, "that I must at once ask you to accept forty-five centimes on the strength of it."

"A beautiful day, monsieur," said the head waiter, rubbing his hands, "I trust that monsieur has slept well."

"So well," I answered, "that monsieur must absolutely insist on your accepting seventy-five centimes on the spot. Come, don't deny me. This is personal matter. Every time I sleep I simply have to give money away."

"Monsieur is most kind."

Kind? I should think not. If the valet de

chambre and the maître d'hôtel and the chef de service and the others of the ten men needed to supply me with fifteen cents worth of coffee, could read my heart, they would find it an abyss of the blackest hatred.

Yet they take their handful of coppers—great grown men dressed up in monkey suits of black at eight in the morning—and bow double for it.

If they tell you it is a warm morning, you must give them two cents. If you ask the time, it costs you two cents. If you want a real genuine burst of conversation, it costs anywhere from a cent to a cent and a half a word.

Such is Paris all day long. Tip, tip, tip, till the brain is weary, not with the cost of it, but with the arithmetical strain.

No pleasure is perfect. Every rose has its thorn. The thorn of the Parisian holiday-maker is the perpetual necessity of handing out small gratuities to a set of overgrown flunkies too lazy to split wood.

Not that the amount of the tips, all added together, is anything serious. No rational man would grudge it if it could be presented in a bill as a lump sum at breakfast time every morning and done with for the day.

But the incessant necessity of handing out small tips of graded amounts gets on one's nerves. It is necessary in Paris to go round with enough money of different denominations in one's pocket to start a bank—gold and paper notes for serious purchases, and with them a huge dead weight of great silver pieces, five franc bits as large as a Quaker's shoebuckle, and a jingling mass of coppers in a side pocket. These one must distribute as extras to cabmen, waiters, news-vendors, beggars, anybody and everybody in fact that one has anything to do with.

The whole mass of the coppers carried only amounts perhaps to twenty-five cents in honest Canadian money. But the silly system of the French currency makes the case appear worse than it is, and gives one the impression of being a walking treasury.

Morning, noon, and night the visitor is perpetually putting his hand into his side pocket and pulling out coppers. He drips coppers all day in an unending stream. You enter a French theatre. You buy a programme, fifty centimes, and ten more to the man who sells it. You hand your coat and cane to an aged harpy, who presides over what is called the vestiaire, pay her twenty-five centimes and give her ten. You are shown to your seat by another old fairy in dingy black (she has a French name, but I forget it) and give her twenty centimes. Just think of the silly business of it. Your ticket, if it is a good seat in a good theatre, has cost you about three dollars and a half. One would almost think the theatre could afford to throw in eight cents worth of harpies for the sake of international good will.

Similarly, in your hotel, you ring the bell and there appears the valet de chambre, dressed in a red waistcoat and a coat effect of black taffeta. You tell him that you want a bath. "Bien, monsieur!" He will fetch the maître d'hôtel. Oh, he will, will he, how good of him, but really one can't witness such kindness on his part without begging him to accept a twenty-five centime remembrance. "Merci bien, monsieur." The maître d'hôtel comes. He is a noble looking person who wears a dress suit at eight o'clock in the morning with patent leather shoes of the kind that I have always wanted but am still unable to afford. Yet I know from experience that the man merely lives and breathes at fifty centimes a breath. For fifty centimes he'll bow low enough to crack himself. If you gave him a franc, he'd lie down on the floor and lick your boots. I know he would; I've seen them do it.

So when the news comes that you propose to take a bath, he's right along side of you in a minute, all civility. Mind you, in a really French hotel, one with what is called the old French atmosphere, taking a bath is quite an event, and the maître d'hôtel sees a dead sure fifty centimes in it, with perhaps an extra ten centimes if times are good. That is to say, he may clear anything from ten to twelve cents on the transaction. A bath, monsieur? Nothing more simple, this moment, tout de suite, right off, he will at once give orders for it. So you give him eleven cents and he then tells the hotel harpy, dressed in black, like the theatre harpies, to get the bath and she goes and gets it. She was there, of course, all the time, right in the corridor, and heard all that proceeded, but she doesn't "enter into her functions" until the valet de chambre tells the maître d'hôtel and the maître d'hôtel informs her officially of the coming event.

She gets the bath. What does she do? Why, merely opens the door of the bathroom, which wasn't locked, and turns on the water. But, of course, no man with any chivalry in him could allow a harpy to be put to all that labour without pressing her to accept three cents as a mark of personal appreciation.

Thus the maître d'hôtel and the valet de chambre and the harpy go on all day, from six in the morning when they first "enter into functions" until heaven knows when at night when they leave off, and they keep gathering in two cents and three cents and even five cents at a time. Then presently, I suppose, they go off and spend it in their own way. The maître d'hôtel transformed into a cheap Parisian with a dragon-fly coat and a sixty cent panama, dances gaily at the Bal Wagram, and himself hands out coppers to the musicians, and gives a one cent tip to a lower order of maître d'hôtel. The harpy goes forth, and with other harpies absorbs red wine and indescribable cheese at eleven at night in a crowded little café on the crowded sidewalk of a street about as wide as a wagon. She tips the waiter who serves her at the rate of one cent per half hour of attendance, and he, I suppose, later on tips someone else, and so on endlessly.

In this way about fifty thousand people in Paris eke out a livelihood by tipping one another.

The worst part of the tipping system is that very often the knowledge that tips are expected and the uncertainty of their amount, causes one to forego a great number of things that might otherwise be enjoyable.

I brought with me to Paris, for example, a letter of introduction to the President of the Republic. I don't say this in any boasting spirit. A university professor can always get all the letters of introduction that he wants. Everyone knows that he is too simple to make any commercial use of them. But I never presented this letter to the President. What was the use? It wouldn't have been worth it. He would have expected a tip, and of course in his case it would have had to be a liberal one, twenty-five cents straight out. Perhaps, too, some of his ministers would have strolled in, as soon as they saw a stranger, on the chance of picking up something. Put it as three ministers at fifteen cents each, that's forty-five cents or a total of seventy cents for ten minutes' talk with the French Government. It's not worth it.

In all Paris, I only found one place where tipping is absolutely out of the question. That was at the British Embassy. There they don't allow it. Not only the clerks and the secretaries, but even the Ambassador himself is forbidden to take so much as the smallest gratuity.

And they live up to it.

That is why I still feel proud of having made an exception to the rule.

I went there because the present ambassador is a personal friend of mine. I hadn't known this till I went to Paris, and I may say in fairness that we are friends no longer: as soon as I came away, our friendship seemed to have ceased.

I will make no secret of the matter. I wanted permission to read in the National Library in Paris. All Frenchmen are allowed to read there and, in addition, all the personal friends of the foreign ambassadors. By a convenient fiction, everybody is the friend of this ambassador, and is given a letter to prove it, provided he will call at the Embassy and get it. That is how I came to be a friend of the British Ambassador. Whether our friendship will ripen into anything warmer and closer, it is not for me to say.

But I went to the Embassy.

The young man that I dealt with was, I think, a secretary. He was—I could see it at once—that perfect thing called an English gentleman. I have seldom seen, outside of baseball circles, so considerate a manner. He took my card, and from sheer considerateness left me alone for half an hour. Then he came back for a moment and said it was a glorious day. I had heard this phrase so often in Paris that I reached into my pocket for ten cents. But something in the quiet dignity of the young man held me back. So I merely answered that it was indeed a glorious day, and that the crops would soon head out nicely if we got this sunshine, provided there wasn't dew enough to start the rust, in which case I was afraid that if an early frost set in we might be badly fooled. He said "indeed," and asked me if I had read the last London *Weekly Times*. I said that I had not seen the last one; but that I had read one about a year ago and that it seemed one of the most sparkling things I had ever read; I had simply roared over it from cover to cover.

He looked pleased and went away.

When he came back, he had the letter of commendation in his hand.

Would you believe it? The civility of it! They had printed the letter, every word of it —except my own name—and it explained all about the ambassador and me being close friends, and told of his desire to have me read in the National Library.

I took the letter, and I knew of course that the moment had come to do something handsome for the young man. But he looked so calm that I still hesitated.

I took ten cents out of my pocket and held it where the light could glitter from every point of its surface full in his face.

And I said——

"My dear young friend, I hope I don't insult you. You are, I can see it, an English gentleman. Your manner betrays it. I, too, though I may seem only what I am, had I not been brought up in Toronto, might have been like you. But enough of this weakness,—will you take ten cents?"

He hesitated. He looked all round. I could see that he was making a great effort. The

Something in the quiet dignity of the young man held me.

spirit of Paris battled against his better nature. He was tempted, but he didn't fall.

"I'm sorry, sir," he said. "I'd like to take it, but I'm afraid I mustn't."

"Young man," I said, "I respect your feelings. You have done me a service. If you ever fall into want and need a position in the Canadian Cabinet, or a seat in our Senate, let me know at once."

I left him.

Then by an odd chance, as I passed to the outer door, there was the British Ambassador himself. He was standing beside the door waiting to open it. There was no mistaking him. I could tell by his cocked hat and brass buttons and the brass chain across his chest that it was the Ambassador. The way in which he swung the door back and removed his hat showed him a trained diplomat.

The moment had come. I still held my ten cents.

"My lord," I said, "I understand your position as the only man in Paris who must not accept a tip, but I insist."

I slipped the money into his hand.

"Thank'ee kindly, sir," said the Ambassador.

Diplomatically speaking, the incident was closed.

III.—The Simple Life in Paris

PARIS—at least the Paris of luxury and fashion—is a childless city. Its streets are thronged all day with a crowd that passes in endless succession but with never a child among them. You may stand on the boulevards and count a thousand grown-up persons for one child that goes by.

The case, of course, is not so extreme in the quieter parts of the city. I have seen children, sometimes two or three together, in the Champs Elysées. In the garden of the Tuileries I once saw six all in a group. They seemed to be playing. A passer-by succeeded in getting a snapshot of them without driving them away. In the poorer districts, there are any quantity of children, even enough to sell, but in the Paris of the rich, the child is conspicuous by its absence. The foreign visitors come without their children. The true Parisian lady has pretty well gone out of the business.

Here and there you may see driving past with its mother in an open barouche, or parading the Rue de la Paix on the hand of its nurse, the doll-like substitute for old-time infancy, the fashionable Parisian child. As far as the sex can be determined by looking at it, it is generally a girl. It is dressed in the height of fashion. A huge picture hat reaches out in all directions from its head. Long gloves encase its little arms to prevent it from making a free use of them. A dainty coat of powder on its face preserves it from the distorting effect of a smile. Its little hundred dollar frock reaches down in a sweet simplicity of outline. It has a belt that runs round its thighs to divide it into two harmonious parts. Below that are bare pink legs ending in little silk socks at a dollar an inch and wee slippers clasped with a simple emerald buckle. Therein, of course, the child only obeys the reigning fashion. Simplicity,—so I am informed by the last number of *La Mode Parisienne,*—is the dominant note of Parisian dress to-day,—simplicity, plainness, freedom from all display.

A French lady wears in her hair at the Opera a single, simple tiara bound with a plain row of solitaire diamonds. It is so exquisitely simple in its outline that you can see the single diamonds sticking out from it and can count up the price of each. The Parisian gentleman wears in his button-hole merely a single orchid, —not half a dozen,—and pins his necktie with one plain, ordinary ruby, set in a perfectly unostentatious sunburst of sapphires. There is no doubt of the superiority of this Parisian simplicity. To me, when it broke upon me in reading *La Mode Parisienne,* it came as a kind of inspiration. I took away the stuffy black ribbon with its stupidly elaborate knot from my Canadian Christie hat and wound a single black ostrich feather about it fastened with just the plainest silver aigrette. When I had put that on and pinned a piece of old lace to the tail of my coat with just one safety pin, I walked the street with the quiet dignity of a person whose one idea is not to be conspicuous.

But this is a digression. The child, I was saying, wears about two hundred worth of visible clothing upon it; and I believe that if you were to take it up by its ten-dollar slipper and hold it upside down, you would see about fifty dollars more. The French child has been converted into an elaborately dressed doll. It is altogether a thing of show, an appendage of its fashionably dressed mother, with frock and parasol to match. It is no longer a child, but a living toy or plaything.

Even on these terms the child is not a success. It has a rival who is rapidly beating it off the ground. This is the Parisian dog. As an implement of fashion, as a set-off to the fair sex, as the recipient of ecstatic kisses and ravishing hugs, the Parisian dog can give the child forty points in a hundred and win out. It can dress better, look more intelligent, behave better, bark better,—in fact, the child is simply not in it.

This is why, I suppose, in the world of Parisian luxury, the dog is ousting the infant altogether. You will see, as I said, no children on the boulevards and avenues. You will see dogs by the hundred. Every motor or open

The Parisian dog.

barouche that passes up the Champs Elysées, with its little white cloud of fluffy parasols and garden-hats, has a dainty, beribboned dog sitting among its occupants: in every avenue and promenade you will see hundreds of clipped poodles and toy spaniels; in all the fashionable churches you will see dogs bowed at their devotions.

It was a fair struggle. The child had its chance and was beaten. The child couldn't dress: the dog could. The child couldn't or wouldn't pray: the dog could,—or at least he learnt how. No doubt it came awkwardly at first, but he set himself to it till nowadays a French dog can enter a cathedral with just as much reverence as his mistress, and can pray in the corner of the pew with the same humility as hers. When you get to know the Parisian dogs, you can easily tell a Roman Catholic dog from a Low Church Anglican. I knew a dog once that was converted,—everybody said from motives of policy,—from a Presbyterian, —but, stop, it's not fair to talk about it,—the dog is dead now, and it's not right to speak ill of its belief, no matter how mistaken it may have been.

However, let that pass, what I was saying was that between the child and the dog, each had its chance in a fair open contest and the child is nowhere.

People, who have never seen, even from the outside, the Parisian world of fashion, have no idea to what an extent it has been invaded by the dog craze. Dogs are driven about in motors and open carriages. They are elaborately clipped and powdered and beribboned by special "coiffeurs." They wear little buckled coats and blankets, and in motors,—I don't feel quite sure of this,—they wear motor goggles. There are at least three or four—and for all I know there may be more—fashionable shops in Paris for dogs' supplies. There is one that any curious visitor may easily find at once in the Rue des Petits Champs close to the Avenue de l'Opera. There is another one midway in the galleries of the Palais Royal. In these shops you will see, in the first place, the chains, collars, and whips that are marks of the servitude in which dogs still live (though, by the way, there are already, I think, dog suffragettes heading a very strong movement). You will see also the most delicious, fashionable dog coats, very, very simple, fastened in front with one silver clasp, only one. In the Palais Royal shop they advertise, "Newest summer models for 1913 in dogs' tailoring." There are also dogs' beds made in wickerwork in cradle shape with eider-down coverlets worked over with silk.

A little while ago, the New York papers were filled with an account of a dog's lunch given at the Vanderbilt Hotel by an ultra-fashionable American lady. It was recorded that Vi Sin, the Pekin Spaniel of Mrs. H. of New York, was host to about ten thousand dollars worth of "smart" dogs. I do not know whether or not this story is true, for I only read it in the Parisian papers. But certain it is that the episode would have made no sensation in Paris. A dog eating in a restaurant is a most ordinary spectacle. Only a few days ago I had lunch with a dog,—a very quiet, sensible Belgian poodle, very simply dressed in a plain morning stomach coat of ultramarine with leather insertions. I took quite a fancy to him. When I say that I had lunch with him, I ought to explain that he had a lady, his mistress, with him,—that also is quite usual in Paris. But I didn't know her, and she sat on the further side of him, so that I confined myself to ordinary table civilities with the dog. I was having merely a plain omelette, from motives of economy, and the dog had a little dish of *entrecote d'agneau aux asperges maître d'hôtel.* I took some of it while the lady was speaking to the waiter and found it excellent. You may believe it or not, but the entry of a dog into a French restaurant and his being seated at a table and having his food ordered creates not the slightest sensation. To bring a child into a really good restaurant would, I imagine, be looked upon as rather a serious affair.

Not only is the dog the darling of the hour during his lifetime, but even in death he is not forgotten. There is in Paris a special dog cemetery. It lies among the drooping trees of a little island in the Seine, called the Isle de la Recette, and you may find it by taking the suburban tramway for Asnières. It has little tombstones, monuments, and flowered walks. One sorrow-stricken master has inscribed over a dog's grave,—*"Plus je vois les hommes, plus j'aime mon chien."* The most notable feature of the cemetery is the monument of Barry, a St. Bernard dog. The inscription states that he saved forty lives in the Alps.

But the dog craze is after all only a sign and sample of the prevailing growth and extent of fashionable luxury. Nowhere in the world, I suppose, is this more conspicuous than in Paris, the very Vanity Fair of mundane pleasure. The hostesses of dinners, dances and fêtes vie with one another in seeking bizarre and extravagant effects. Here is a good example of it taken from actual life the other day. It is an account of an "oriental fête" given at a private mansion in Paris.

It runs thus:—"The sumptuous Paris mansion of the Comtesse Aynard de Chabrillan in the Rue Christophe-Colomb was converted into a veritable scene from the 'Thousand and One Nights' on the occasion of a Persian fête given by her to a large company of friends.

"In the courtyard an immense tent was erected, hung with superb Persian stuffs and tapestries, and here the élite of Paris assembled in gorgeous Oriental costumes.

"The countess herself presided in a magnificent Persian costume of green and gold, with an immense white aigrette in her hair."

Notice it. The simplicity of it! Only green and gold in her costume, no silver, no tin, no galvanized iron, just gold, plain gold; and only "one immense white aigrette." The quiet dignity of it!

The article goes on:—"Each of the sensational entries was announced by M. André de Fouquières, the arbiter of Parisian elegance.

"One of the most striking spectacles of the evening was the appearance of Princesse P. d'Arenberg, mounted on an elephant, richly bedecked with Indian trappings. Then came the Duchesse de Clermont-Tonnerre and the

Comtesse Stanislas de Castellane in gold cages, followed by the Marquise de Brantes, in a flower-strewn Egyptian litter, accompanied by Pharaoh and his slaves.

"The Comtesse de Lubersac danced an Oriental measure with charming grace, and Prince Luis Fernando of Spain, in an ethereal costume, his features stained a greenish hue, executed a Hindoo dance before the assembly."

Can you beat it? His features stained with a greenish hue! Now look at that! He might have put on high grade prepared paint or clear white lead,—he's rich enough,—but, no, just a quiet shingle stain is enough for him.

I cannot resist adding from the same source the list of the chief guests. Anybody desiring a set of names for a burlesque show to run three hundred nights on the circuit may have them free of charge or without infringement of copyright.

"Nearly everyone prominent in Paris society was present, including the Maharajah of Kapurthala, Princess Prem Kaur, Prince Aga Khan, the Austrian Ambassador and Countess

Szecsen, the Persian and Bulgarian Ministers, Mme. Stancioff, Duc and Duchesse de Noailles, Comtesse A. Potocka, Marquis and Marquise de Mun, Comtesse du Bourg de Bozas, Mrs. Moore, Comte and Comtesse G. de Segonzec and Prince and Princess de Croy."

I am sorry that "Mrs. Moore" was there. She must have slipped in unnoticed.

What is not generally known is that I was there myself. I appeared,—in rivalry with Prince Luis Fernando—dressed as a Bombay soda water bottle, with aerial opalescent streaks of light flashing from the costume which was bound with single wire.

IV.—A Visit to Versailles

"WHAT!" said the man from Kansas, looking up from his asparagus, "do you mean to say that you have never seen the Palace of Versailles?"

"No," I said very firmly, "I have not."

"Nor the fountains in the gardens?"

"No."

"Nor the battle pictures?"

"No."

"And the Hall of Mirrors,"—added the fat lady from Georgia.

"And Madame du Barry's bed"—said her husband.

"Her which," I asked, with some interest.

"Her bed."

"All right," I said, "I'll go."

I knew, of course, that I had to. Every tourist in Paris has got to go and see Versailles. Otherwise the superiority of the others becomes insufferable, with foreigners it is different. If they worry one about palaces and cathedrals and such—the Château at Versailles, and the Kaiserhof and the Duomo at Milan—I answer them in kind. I ask them if they have ever seen the Schlitzerhof at Milwaukee and the Anheuserbusch at St. Louis, and the Dammo at Niagara, and the Toboggo at Montreal. That quiets them wonderfully.

But, as I say, I had to go.

You get to Versailles—as the best of various ways of transport—by means of a contrivance something between a train and a street car. It has a little puffing steam-engine and two cars—double deckers—with the top deck open to the air and covered with a wooden roof on rods. The lower part inside is called the first-class and a seat in it costs ten cents extra. Otherwise nobody would care to ride in it. The engine is a quaint little thing and wears a skirt, painted green, all around it, so that you can just see the tips of its wheels peeping modestly out below. It was a great relief to me to see this engine. It showed that there is such a thing as French delicacy after all. There are so many sights along the boulevards that bring the carmine blush to the face of the tourist (from the twisting of his neck in trying to avoid seeing them), that it is well to know that the French draw the line somewhere. The sight of the bare wheels of an engine is too much for them.

The little train whirls its way out of Paris, past the great embankment and the fortifications, and goes rocking along among green trees whose branches sweep its sides, and trim villas with stone walls around quaint gardens. At every moment it passes little inns and suburban restaurants with cool arbours in front of them, and waiters in white coats pouring out glasses of red wine. It makes one thirsty just to look at them.

In due time the little train rattles and rocks itself over the dozen miles or so that separate Paris from Versailles, and sets you down right in front of the great stone court-yard of the palace. There through the long hours of a summer afternoon you may feast your eyes upon the wonderland of beauty that rose at the command of the grand monarch, Louis XIV, from the sanded plains and wooded upland that marked the spot two hundred and fifty years ago.

All that royal munificence could effect was lavished on the making of the palace. So vast is it in size that in the days of its greatest splendour it harboured ten thousand inmates. The sheer length of it from side to side is only about a hundred yards short of half a mile. To make the grounds the King's chief landscape artist and his hundreds of workers laboured for twenty years. They took in, as it were, the whole landscape. The beauty of their work lies not only in the wonderful terraces, gardens, groves and fountains that extend from the rear of the Château, but in its blending with the scene beyond. It is so planned that no distant house or building breaks into the picture. The vista ends everywhere with the waving woods of the purple distance.

Louis XIV spent in all, they say, a hundred

million dollars on the making of the palace. When made it was filled with treasures of art not to be measured in price. It was meant to be, and it remains, the last word of royal grandeur. The King's court at Versailles became the sun round which gravitated the fate and fortune of his twenty million subjects. Admission within its gates was itself a mark of royal favour. Now, any person with fifteen cents may ride out from Paris on the double-decked street car and wander about the palace at will. For a five cent tip to a guide you may look through the private apartments of Marie Antoinette, and for two cents you may check your umbrella while you inspect the bedroom of Napoleon the First. For nothing at all you may stand on the vast terrace behind the Château and picture to yourself the throng of gay ladies in paniered skirts, and powdered gentlemen, in sea-green inexpressibles, who walked among its groves and fountains two hundred years ago. The palace of the Kings has become the playground of the democracy.

The palace—or the Château, as it is modestly named—stands crosswise upon an elevation that dominates the scene for miles around. The whole building throughout is only of three stories, for French architecture has a horror of high buildings. The two great wings of the Château reach sideways, north and south; and one, a shorter one, runs westwards towards the rear. In the front space between the wings is a vast paved court-yard—the Royal Court—shut in by a massive iron fence. Into this court penetrated, one autumn evening in 1789, the raging mob led by the women of Paris, who had come to drag the descendant of the Grand Monarch into the captivity that ended only with the guillotine. Here they lighted their bonfires and here they sang and shrieked and shivered throughout the night. That night of the fifth of October was the real end of monarchy in France.

No one, I think—not even my friend from Kansas who boasted that he had "put in" three hours at Versailles—could see all that is within the Château. But there are certain things which no tourist passes by. One of them is the suite of rooms of Louis XIV, a great series of square apartments all opening sideways into each other with gilded doors as large as those of a barn, and with about as much privacy as a railway station. One room was the King's council chamber; next to this, a larger one, was the "wig-room," where the royal mind selected its wig for the day and where the royal hair-dresser performed his stupendous task. Besides this again is the King's bedroom. Preserved in it, within a little fence, still stands the bed in which Louis XIV died in 1715, after a reign of seventy-two years. The bedroom would easily hold three hundred people. Outside of it is a great antechamber, where the courtiers jealously waited their turn to be present at the King's "lever," or "getting up," eager to have the supreme honour of holding the royal breeches.

But if the King's apartments are sumptuous, they are as nothing to the Hall of Mirrors, the showroom of the whole palace, and estimated to be the most magnificent single room in the world. It extends clear across the end of the rear wing and has a length of 236 feet. It is lighted by vast windows that reach almost to the lofty arch that forms its ceiling; the floor is of polished inlaid wood, on which there stood in Louis the Great's time, tables, chairs, and other furniture of solid silver. The whole inner side of the room is formed by seventeen enormous mirrors set in spaces to correspond in shape to the window opposite, and fitted in between with polished marble. Above them runs a cornice of glittering gilt, and over that again the ceiling curves in a great arch, each panel of it bearing some picture to recall the victories of the Grand Monarch. Ungrateful posterity has somewhat forgotten the tremendous military achievements of Louis XIV—the hardships of his campaign in the Netherlands in which the staff of the royal cusine was cut down to one hundred cooks—the passage of the Rhine, in which the King actually crossed the river from one side to the other, and so on. But the student of history can live again the triumphs of Louis in this Hall of Mirrors. It is an irony of history that in this room, after the conquest of 1871, the King of Prussia was proclaimed German Emperor by his subjects and his allies.

But if one wants to see battle pictures, one has but to turn to the north wing of the Château. There you have them, room after room—twenty, thirty, fifty roomsful—I don't know how many—the famous gallery of battles, depicting the whole military history of France from the days of King Clovis till the French Revolution. They run in historical order. The pictures begin with battles of early barbarians—men with long hair wielding huge battle-axes with their eyes blazing, while other barbarians prod at them with pikes or take a sweep at them with a two-handed club. After that there are rooms full of crusade pictures—crusaders fighting the Arabs, crusaders investing Jerusalem, crusaders raising the siege of Malta and others raising the siege of Rhodes; all very picturesque, with the blue Mediterranean, the yellow sand of the desert, prancing steeds in nickel-plated armour and knights plumed and caparisoned, or whatever it is, and wearing as many crosses as an ambulance emergency staff. All of these battles were apparently quite harmless, that is the strange thing about these battle pictures: the whole thing, as depicted for the royal eye, is wonderfully full of colour and picturesque, but, as far as one can see, quite harmless. Nobody seems to be getting hurt, wild-looking men are swinging maces round, but you can see that they won't hit anybody. A battle-axe is being brought down with terrific force, but somebody is thrusting up a steel shield just in time to meet it. There are no signs of blood or injury. Everybody seems to be getting along finely and to be having the most invigorating physical exercise. Here and here, perhaps, the artist depicts somebody jammed down under a beam or lying under the feet of a horse; but if you look close you see that the beam isn't really pressing on him, and that the horse is not really stepping on his stomach. In fact the man is perfectly comfortable, and is, at the moment, taking aim at somebody else with a two-string crossbow, which would have deadly effect if he wasn't ass enough to aim right at the middle of a cowhide shield.

You notice this quality more and more in the pictures as the history moves on. After the invention of gunpowder, when the combatants didn't have to be locked together, but could be separated by fields, and little groves and quaint farm-houses, the battle seems to get quite lost in the scenery. It spreads out into the landscape until it becomes one of the prettiest, quietest scenes that heart could wish. I know nothing so drowsily comfortable as the pictures in this gallery that show the battles of the seventeenth century,—the Grand Monarch's own particular epoch. This is a wide, rolling landscape with here and there little clusters of soldiers to add a touch of colour to the foliage of the woods; there are woolly little puffs of smoke rising in places to show that the artillery is at its dreamy work on a hill side; near the foreground is a small group of generals standing about a tree and gazing through glasses at the dim purple of the background. There are sheep and cattle grazing in all the unused parts of the battle, the whole thing has a touch of quiet, rural feeling that goes right to the heart. I have seen people from the ranching district of the Middle West stand before these pictures in tears.

It is strange to compare this sort of thing with some of the modern French pictures. There is realism enough and to spare in them. In the Salon exhibition a year or two ago, for instance, there was one that represented lions turned loose into an arena to eat up Christians. I can imagine exactly how a Louis Quatorze artist would have dealt with the subject,—an arena, prettily sanded, with here and there gooseberry bushes and wild gilly flowers (not too wild, of course), lions with flowing manes, in noble attitudes, about to roar,—tigers, finely developed, about to spring, —Christians just going to pray,—and through it all a genial open-air feeling very soothing to the royal senses. Not so the artist of to-day. The picture in the Salon is of blood. There are torn limbs gnawed by crouching beasts, as a dog holds and gnaws a bone; there are faces being torn, still quivering, from the writhing body,—in fact, perhaps after all there is something to be said for the way the Grand Monarch arranged his gallery.

The battle pictures and the Hall of Mirrors, and the fountains and so on, are, I say, the things best worth seeing at Versailles. Everybody says so. I really wish now that I had seen them. But I am free to confess that I am a poor sightseer at the best. As soon as I get actually in reach of a thing it somehow dwindles in importance. I had a friend once, now a distinguished judge in the United States, who suffered much in this way. He travelled a thousand miles to reach the World's Fair, but as soon as he had arrived at a comfortable hotel in Chicago, he was unable to find the energy to go out to the Fair grounds. He went once to visit Niagara Falls, but failed to see the actual water, partly because it no longer seemed necessary, partly because his room in the hotel looked the other way.

Personally I plead guilty to something of the same spirit. Just where you alight from the steam tramway at Versailles, you will find close on your right, a little open-air café, with tables under a trellis of green vines. It is as cool a retreat of mingled sun and shadow as I know. There is red wine at two francs and long imported cigars of as soft a flavour as even Louis the Fourteenth could have desired. The idea of leaving a grotto like that to go trapesing all over a hot stuffy palace with a lot of fool tourists, seemed ridiculous. But I bought there a little illustrated book called the *Château de Versailles,* which interested me so extremely that I decided that, on some reasonable opportunity, I would go and visit the place.

Personally I plead guilty to something of the same spirit.

V.—*Paris at Night*

WHAT Ah'd like to do," says the Fat Lady from Georgia, settling back comfortably in her seat after her five-dollar dinner at the Café American, while her husband is figuring whether ten francs is enough to give to the waiter, "is to go and see something real wicked. Ah tell him (the word 'him' is used in Georgia to mean husband) that while we're here Ah just want to see everything that's going."

"All right," says the Man from Kansas who "knows" Paris, "I'll get a guide right here, and he'll take us round and show us the sights."

"Can you get him heah?" asks the gentleman from Georgia, looking round at the glittering mirrors and gold cornices of the restaurant.

Can you get a guide? Well, now! Can you keep away from them? All day from the dewy hour of breakfast till late at night they meet you in the street and sidle up with the enquiry, "Guide, sir?"

Where the Parisian guide comes from and how he graduates for his job I do not know. He is not French and, as a rule, he doesn't know Paris. He knows his way to the Louvre and to two or three American bars and to the Moulin Rouge in Montmartre. But he doesn't need to know his way. For that he falls back on the taxi-driver. "Now, sir," says the guide briskly to the gentleman who has engaged his services, "where would you like to go?" "I should like to see Napoleon's tomb." "All right," says the guide, "get into the taxi." Then he turns to the driver. "Drive to Napoleon's tomb," he says. After they have looked at it the guide says, "What would you like to see next, sir?" "I am very anxious to see Victor Hugo's house, which I understand is now made open to the public." The guide turns to the taxi man. "Drive to Victor Hugo's house," he says.

After looking through the house the visitor

says in a furtive way, "I was just wondering if I could get a drink anywhere in this part of the town?" "Certainly," says the guide. "Drive to an American bar."

Isn't that simple? Can you imagine any more agreeable way of earning five dollars in three hours than that? Of course, what the guide says to the taxi man is said in the French language, or in something resembling it, and the gentleman in the cab doesn't understand it. Otherwise, after six or seven days of driving round in this way he begins to wonder what the guide is for. But of course, the guide's life, when you come to think of it, is one full of difficulty and danger. Just suppose that, while he was away off somewhere in Victor Hugo's house or at Napoleon's grave, the taxi-driver were to be struck by lightning. How on earth would he get home? He might, perhaps, be up in the Eiffel Tower and the taxi man get a stroke of paralysis, and then he'd starve to death trying to find his way back. After all, the guide has to have the kind of pluck and hardihood that ought to be well rewarded. Why, in other countries, like Switzerland, they have to use dogs for it, and in France, when these plucky fellows throw themselves into it, surely one wouldn't grudge the nominal fee of five dollars for which they risk their lives.

But I am forgetting about the Lady from Georgia and her husband. Off they go in due course from the glittering doors of the restaurant in a huge taxi with a guide in a peaked hat. The party is all animation. The lady's face is aglow with moral enthusiasm. The gentleman and his friend have their coats buttoned tight to their chins for fear that thieves might leap over the side of the taxi and steal their neckties.

So they go buzzing along the lighted boulevard looking for "something real wicked." What they want is to see something really and truly wicked; they don't know just what, but "something bad." They've got the idea that Paris is one of the wickedest places on earth, and they want to see it.

Strangely enough, in their own home, the

The lady's face is aglow with moral enthusiasm

Lady from Georgia is one of the leaders of the Social Purity movement, and her husband, whose skin at this moment is stretched as tight as a football with French brandy and soda, is one of the finest speakers on the Georgia temperance platform, with a reputation that reaches from Chattanooga to Chickamauga. They have a son at Yale College whom they are trying to keep from smoking cigarettes. But here in Paris, so they reckon it, everything is different. It doesn't occur to them that perhaps it is wicked to pay out a hundred dollars in an evening hiring other people to be wicked.

So off they go and are whirled along in the brilliant glare of the boulevards and up the gloomy, narrow streets that lead to Montmartre. They visit the Moulin Rouge and the Bal Tabarin, and they see the Oriental Dances and the Café of Hell and the hundred and one other glittering fakes and false appearances that poor old meretricious Paris works overtime to prepare for such people as themselves. And the Lady from Georgia, having seen it all, thanks Heaven that she at least is pure—which is a beginning—and they go home more enthusiastic than ever in the Social Purity movement.

But the fact is that if you have about twenty-five thousand new visitors pouring into a great city every week with their pockets full of money and clamoring for "something wicked," you've got to do the best you can for them.

Hence it results that Paris—in appearance, anyway—is a mighty gay place at night. The sidewalks are crowded with the little tables of the coffee and liqueur drinkers. The music of a hundred orchestras bursts forth from the lighted windows. The air is soft with the fragrance of a June evening, tempered by the curling smoke of fifty thousand cigars. Through the noise and chatter of the crowd there sounds unending the wail of the motor horn.

The hours of Parisian gaiety are late. Ordinary dinner is eaten at about seven o'clock, but fashionable dinners begin at eight or eight thirty. Theatres open at a quarter to nine and really begin at nine o'clock. Special features and acts,—famous singers and vaudeville artists—are brought on at eleven o'clock so that dinner-party people may arrive in time to see them. The theatres come out at midnight. After that there are the night suppers which flourish till two or half past. But if you wish, you can go between the theater and supper to some such side-long place as the Moulin Rouge or the Bal Tabarin, which reach the height of their supposed merriment at about one in the morning.

At about two or two thirty the motors come whirling home, squawking louder than ever, with a speed limit of fifty miles an hour. Only the best of them can run faster than that. Quiet, conservative people in Paris like to get to bed at three o'clock; after all, what is the use of keeping late hours and ruining one's health and complexion? If you make it a strict rule to be in bed by three, you feel all the better for it in the long run—health better, nerves steadier, eyes clearer—and you're able to get up early—at half-past eleven—and feel fine.

Those who won't or don't go to bed at three wander about the town, eat a second supper in an all-night restaurant, circulate round with guides, and visit the slums of the Market, where gaunt-eyed wretches sleep in crowded alleys in the mephitic air of a summer night, and where the idle rich may feed their luxurious curiosity on the sufferings of the idle poor.

The dinners, the theaters, the boulevards, and the rest of it are all fun enough, at any rate for one visit in a lifetime. The "real wicked" part of it is practically fake—served up for the curious foreigner with money to throw away. The Moulin Rouge whirls the wide sails of its huge sign, crimson with electric bulbs, amid the false glaze of the Place Blanche. Inside of it there is more red—the full red of bad claret and the bright red of congested faces and painted cheeks. Part of the place is a theater with a vaudeville show much like any other. Another part is a vast "promenoir" where you may walk up and down or sit at a little table and drink bad brandy at one franc and a half. In a fenced off part are the Oriental Dances, a familiar feature of every Parisian Show. These dances —at twenty cents a turn—are supposed to represent all the languishing allurement of the Oriental houri—I think that is the word. The dancers in Paris—it is only fair to state—have never been nearer to the Orient than the Faubourg St. Antoine, where they were brought up and where they learned all the Orientalism that they know. Their "dance" is performed with their feet continuously on the ground—never lifted, I mean—and is done by gyrations of the stomach, beside which the paroxysms of an overdose of Paris green are child's play. In seeing these dances one realizes all the horrors of life in the East.

Not everyone, however, can be an Oriental dancer in a French pleasure show. To qualify you must be as scrawny as a Parisian cab-horse, and it appears as if few débutantes could break into the profession under the age of forty. The dances go on at intervals till two in the morning, after which the Oriental houri crawls to her home at the same time as the Parisian cab-horse—her companion in arms.

Under the Moulin Rouge, and in all similar places, is a huge dancc hall: It has a "Hungarian Orchestra"—a fact which is proved by the red and green jackets, the tyrolese caps, and by the printed sign which says, "This is a Hungarian Orchestra." I knew that they were Hungarians the night I saw them, because I distinctly heard one of them say, "what t'ell do we play next boys?" The reference to William Tell was obvious. After every four tunes the Orchestra are given a tall stein of beer, and they all stand up and drink it, shouting "Hoch!" or "Ha!" or "Hoo!" or something of the sort. This is supposed to give a high touch of local colour. Everybody knows how Hungarians always shout out loud when they see a glass of beer. I've noticed it again and again in sugar refineries.

The Hungarians have to drink the beer

whether they like it or not—it's part of their contract. I noticed one poor fellow who was playing the long bassoon, and who was doing a double night-shift overtime. He'd had twenty-four pints of beer already, and there were still two hours before closing time. You could tell what he was feeling like by the sobbing of his instrument. But he stood up every now and then and yelled "Hoch!" or "Hiccough!"—or whatever it was—along with the others.

On the big floor in front of the Hungarians the dance goes on. Most of the time the dances are endless waltzes and polkas shared in by the nondescript frequenters of the place, while the tourist visitors sit behind a railing and watch. To look at, the dancing is about as interesting, nothing more or less, than the round dances at a Canadian picnic on the first of July.

Every now and then, to liven things up, comes the can-can. In theory this is a wild dance, breaking out from sheer ebullience of spirit, and shared in by a bevy of merry girls carried away by gaiety and joy of living. In reality the can-can is performed by eight or ten old nags,—ex-Oriental dancers, I should think,—at eighty cents a night. But they are deserving women, and work hard—like all the rest of the brigade in the factory of Parisian gaiety.

After the Moulin Rouge or the Bal Tabarin or such, comes, of course, a visit to one of the night cafés of the Montmartre district. Their names in themselves are supposed to indicate their weird and alluring character—the Café of Heaven, the Café of Nothingness, and,—how dreadful—the Café of Hell. "Montmartre," says one of the latest English writers on Paris, "is the scene of all that is wild, mad, and extravagant. Nothing is too grotesque, too terrible, too eccentric for the Montmartre mind." Fiddlesticks! What he means is that nothing is too damn silly for people to pay to go to see.

Take, for example, the notorious Café of Hell. The portals are low and gloomy. You enter in the dark. A pass-word is given—

"Stranger, who cometh here?"—"More food for worms." You sit and eat among coffins and shrouds. There are muffled figures shuffling around to represent monks in cowls, saints, demons, and apostles. The "Angel Gabriel" watches at the door. "Father Time" moves among the eaters. The waiters are dressed as undertakers. There are skulls and cross-bones in the walls. The light is that of dim tapers. And so on.

And yet I suppose some of the foreign visitors to the Café of Hell think that this is a truly French home scene, and discuss the queer characteristics of the French people suggested by it.

I got to know a family in Paris that worked in one of these Montmartre night cafés—quiet, decent people they were, with a little home of their own in the suburbs. The father worked as Beelzebub mostly, but he could double with St. Anthony and do a very fair St. Luke when it was called for. The mother worked as Mary Magdalene, but had grown so stout that it was hard for her to hold it. There were two boys, one of whom was working as John the Baptist, but had been promised to be promoted to Judas Iscariot in the fall; they were good people, and worked well, but were tired of their present place. Like everyone else they had heard of Canada and thought of coming out. They were very anxious to know what openings there were in their line; whether there would be any call for a Judas Iscariot in a Canadian restaurant, or whether a man would have any chance as St. Anthony in the West.

I told them frankly that these jobs were pretty well filled up.

Listen! It is striking three. The motors are whirling down the asphalt street. The brilliant lights of the boulevard windows are fading out. Here, as in the silent woods of Canada, night comes at last. The restless city of pleasure settles to its short sleep.

THE RETROACTIVE EXISTENCE OF MR. JUGGINS

The Retroactive Existence of Mr. Juggins

I FIRST met Juggins,—really to notice him,—years and years ago as a boy out camping. Somebody was trying to nail up a board on a tree for a shelf and Juggins interfered to help him.

"Stop a minute," he said, "you need to saw the end of that board off before you put it up." Then Juggins looked round for a saw, and when he got it he had hardly made more than a stroke or two with it before he stopped. "This saw," he said, "needs to be filed up a bit." So he went and hunted up a file to sharpen the saw, but found that before he could use the file he needed to put a proper handle on it, and to make a handle he went to look for a sapling in the bush, but to cut the sapling he found that he needed to sharpen up the axe. To do this, of course, he had to fix the grindstone so as to make it run properly. This involved making wooden legs for the grindstone. To do this decently Juggins decided to make a carpenter's bench. This was quite impossible without a better set of tools. Juggins went to the village to get the tools required, and, of course, he never came back.

He was re-discovered—weeks later—in the city, getting prices on wholesale tool machinery.

After that first episode I got to know Juggins very well. For some time we were students at college together. But Juggins somehow never got far with his studies. He always began with great enthusiasm and then something happened. For a time he studied French with tremendous eagerness. But he soon found that for a real knowledge of French you need first to get a thorough grasp of Old French and Provençal. But it proved impossible to do anything with these without an absolutely complete command of Latin. This Juggins discovered could only be obtained, in any thorough way, through Sanskrit, which of course lies at the base of it. So Juggins devoted himself to Sanskrit until he realised that for a proper understanding of Sanskrit one needs to study the ancient Iranian, the root-language underneath. This language however is lost.

So Juggins had to begin over again. He did, it is true, make some progress in natural science. He studied physics and rushed rapidly backwards from forces to molecules, and from molecules to atoms, and from atoms to electrons, and then his whole studies exploded backward into the infinities of space, still searching a first cause.

Juggins, of course, never took a degree, so he made no practical use of his education. But it didn't matter. He was very well off and was able to go straight into business with a capital of about a hundred thousand dollars. He put it at first into a gas plant, but found that he lost money at that because of the high price of the coal needed to make gas. So he sold out for ninety thousand dollars and went into coal mining. This was unsuccessful because of the awful cost of mining machinery. So Juggins sold his share in the mine for eighty thousand dollars and went in for manufacturing mining machinery. At this he would have undoubtedly made money but for the enormous cost of gas needed as motive-power for the plant. Juggins sold out of the manufacture for seventy thousand, and after that he went whirling in a circle, like skating backwards, through the different branches of allied industry.

He lost a certain amount of money each year, especially in good years when trade was brisk. In dull times when everything was unsalable he did fairly well.

Juggins' domestic life was very quiet.

Of course he never married. He did, it is true, fall in love several times; but each time it ended without result. I remember well his first love story for I was very intimate with him at the time. He had fallen in love with the girl in question utterly and immediately.

It was literally love at first sight. There was no doubt of his intentions. As soon as he had met her he was quite frank about it. "I intend," he said, "to ask her to be my wife."

"When?" I asked; "right away?"

"No," he said, "I want first to fit myself to be worthy of her."

So he went into moral training to fit himself. He taught in a Sunday school for six weeks, till he realised that a man has no business in Divine work of that sort without first preparing himself by serious study of the history of Palestine. And he felt that a man was a cad to force his society on a girl while he is still only half acquainted with the history of the Israelites. So Juggins stayed away. It was nearly two years before he was fit to propose. By the time he *was* fit, the girl had already married a brainless thing in patent leather boots who didn't even know who Moses was.

Of course Juggins fell in love again. People always do. And at any rate by this time he was in a state of moral fitness that made it imperative.

So he fell in love—deeply in love this time—with a charming girl, commonly known as the eldest Miss Thorneycroft. She was only called eldest because she had five younger sisters; and she was very poor and awfully clever and trimmed all her own hats. Any man, if he's worth the name, falls in love with that sort of thing at first sight. So, of course, Juggins would have proposed to her; only when he went to the house he met her next sister: and of course she was younger still; and, I suppose, poorer: and made not only her own hats but her own blouses. So Juggins fell in love with her. But one night when he went to call, the door was opened by the sister younger still, who not only made her own blouses and trimmed her own hats, but even made her own tailor-made suits. After that Juggins backed up from sister to sister till he went through the whole family, and in the end got none of them.

Perhaps it was just as well that Juggins

never married. It would have made things very difficult because, of course, he got poorer all the time. You see after he sold out his last share in his last business he bought with it a diminishing life annuity, so planned that he always got rather less next year than this year, and still less the year after. Thus, if he lived long enough, he would starve to death.

Meantime he has become a quaint-looking elderly man, with coats a little too short and trousers a little above his boots—like a boy. His face too is like that of a boy, with wrinkles.

And his talk now has grown to be always reminiscent. He is perpetually telling long stories of amusing times that he has had with different people that he names.

He says for example—

"I remember a rather queer thing that happened to me in a train one day——"

And if you say—"When was that Juggins?" —he looks at you in a vague way as if calculating and says,—"in 1875, or 1876, I think, as near as I recall it—"

I notice, too, that his reminiscences are

going further and further back. He used to base his stories on his recollections as a young man, now they are further back.

The other day he told me a story about himself and two people that he called the Harper brothers,—Ned and Joe. Ned, he said was a tremendously powerful fellow.

I asked how old Ned was and Juggins said that he was three. He added that there was another brother not so old, but a very clever fellow about,—here Juggins paused and calculated—about eighteen months.

So then I realised where Juggins retroactive existence is carrying him to. He has passed back through childhood into infancy, and presently, just as his annuity runs to a point and vanishes, he will back up clear through the Curtain of Existence and die,—or be born, I don't know which to call it.

Meantime he remains to me as one of the most illuminating allegories I have met.

Meanwhile he had become a quaint-looking elderly man.

MAKING A MAGAZINE

(The Dream of a Contributor)

Making a Magazine

I DREAMT one night not long ago that I was the editor of a great illustrated magazine. I offer no apology for this: I have often dreamt even worse of myself than that.

In any case I didn't do it on purpose: very often, I admit, I try to dream that I am President Wilson, or Mr. Bryan, or the Ritz-Carlton Hotel, or a share of stock in the Standard Oil Co. for the sheer luxury and cheapness of it. But this was an accident. I had been sitting up late at night writing personal reminiscences of Abraham Lincoln. I was writing against time. The presidential election was drawing nearer every day and the market for reminiscences of Lincoln was extremely brisk, but, of course, might collapse any moment. Writers of my class have to consider this sort of thing. For instance, in the middle of Lent, I find that I can do fairly well with "Recent Lights on the Scriptures." Then, of course, when the hot weather comes, the market for Christmas poetry opens and there's a fairly good demand for voyages in the Polar Seas. Later on, in the quiet of the autumn I generally write some "Unpublished Letters from Goethe to Balzac," and that sort of thing.

But it's a wearing occupation, full of disappointments, and needing the very keenest business instinct to watch every turn of the market.

I am afraid that this is a digression. I only wanted to explain how a man's mind could be so harassed and overwrought as to make him dream that he was an editor.

I knew at once in my dream where and what I was. As soon as I saw the luxury of the surroundings,—the spacious room with its vaulted ceiling, lit with stained glass,—the beautiful mahogany table at which I sat writing with a ten-dollar fountain pen, the gift of the manufacturers,—on embossed stationery, the gift of the embossers,—on which I was setting down words at eight and a half cents a word and deliberately picking out short ones through sheer business acuteness;—as soon as I saw;—this I said to myself—

"I am an editor, and this is my editorial sanctum." Not that I have ever seen an editor or a sanctum. But I have sent so many manuscripts to so many editors and received them back with such unfailing promptness, that the scene before me was as familiar to my eye as if I had been wide awake.

As I thus mused, revelling in the charm of my surroundings and admiring the luxurious black alpaca coat and the dainty dickie which I wore, there was a knock at the door.

A beautiful creature entered. She evidently belonged to the premises, for she wore no hat and there were white cuffs upon her wrists. She has that indescribable beauty of effectiveness such as is given to hospital nurses.

This, I thought to myself, must be my private secretary.

"I hope I don't interrupt you, sir," said the girl.

"My dear child," I answered, speaking in that fatherly way in which an editor might well address a girl almost young enough to be his wife, "pray do not mention it. Sit down. You must be fatigued after your labours of the morning. Let me ring for a club sandwich."

"I came to say, sir," the secretary went on, "that there's a person downstairs waiting to see you."

My manner changed at once.

"Is he a gentleman or a contributor?" I asked.

"He doesn't look exactly like a gentleman."

"Very good," I said. "He's a contributor for sure. Tell him to wait. Ask the caretaker to lock him in the coal cellar, and kindly slip out and see if there's a policeman on the beat in case I need him."

"Very good, sir," said the secretary.

I waited for about an hour, wrote a few editorials advocating the rights of the people, smoked some Turkish cigarettes, drank a glass of sherry, and ate part of an anchovy sandwich.

Then I rang the bell. "Bring that man here," I said.

Presently they brought him in. He was a timid-looking man with an embarrassed manner and all the low cunning of an author stamped on his features. I could see a bundle of papers in his hand, and I knew that the scoundrel was carrying a manuscript.

"Now, sir," I said, "speak quickly. What's your business?"

"I've got here a manuscript," he began.

"What!" I shouted at him. "A manuscript! You'd dare, would you! Bringing manuscripts in here! What sort of a place do you think this is?"

"It's the manuscript of a story," he faltered.

"A story!" I shrieked. "What on earth do you think we'd want stories for! Do you think we've nothing better to do than to print your idiotic ravings. Have you any idea, you idiot, of the expense we're put to in setting up our fifty pages of illustrated advertising? Look here," I continued, seizing a bundle of proof illustrations that lay in front of me, "do you see this charming picture of an Asbestos Cooker, guaranteed fireless, odourless, and purposeless! Do you see this patent motor-car with pneumatic cushions, and the full-page description of its properties? Can you form any idea of the time and thought that we have to spend on these things, and yet you dare to come in here with your miserable stories. By heaven," I said, rising in my seat, "I've a notion to come over there and choke you: I'm entitled to do it by the law, and I think I will."

"Don't, don't," he pleaded. "I'll go away. I meant no harm. I'll take it with me."

"No you don't," I interrupted; "none of your sharp tricks with this magazine. You've submitted this manuscript to me, and it stays submitted. If I don't like it, I shall prosecute you, and, I trust, obtain full reparation from the courts."

To tell the truth, it had occurred to me that perhaps I might need after all to buy the miserable stuff. Even while I felt that my indignation at the low knavery of the fellow

With all the low cunning of an author stamped on his features.

was justified, I knew that it might be necessary to control it. The present low state of public taste demands a certain amount of this kind of matter distributed among the advertising.

I rang the bell again.

"Please take this man away and shut him up again. Have them keep a good eye on him. He's an author."

"Very good, sir," said the secretary.

I called her back for one moment.

"Don't feed him anything," I said.

"No," said the girl.

The manuscript lay before me on the table. It looked bulky. It bore the title *Dorothy Dacres, or, Only a Clergyman's Daughter.*

I rang the bell again.

"Kindly ask the janitor to step this way."

He came in. I could see from the straight, honest look in his features that he was a man to be relied upon.

"Jones," I said, "can you read?"

"Yes, sir," he said, "some."

"Very good. I want you to take this manuscript and read it. Read it all through and then bring it back here."

The janitor took the manuscript and disappeared. I turned to my desk again and was soon absorbed in arranging a full-page display of plumbers' furnishings for the advertising. It had occurred to me that by arranging the picture matter in a neat device with verses from "Home Sweet Home" running through it in double-leaded old English type, I could set up a page that would be the delight of all business readers and make this number of the magazine a conspicuous success. My mind was so absorbed that I scarcely noticed that over an hour elapsed before the janitor returned.

"Well, Jones," I said as he entered, "have you read that manuscript?"

"Yes, sir."

"And you find it all right—punctuation good, spelling all correct?"

"Very good indeed, sir."

"And there is, I trust, nothing of what one would call a humorous nature in it? I want you to answer me quite frankly, Jones,—there is nothing in it that would raise a smile, or even a laugh, is there?"

"Oh, no, sir," said Jones, "nothing at all."

"And now tell me—for remember that the reputation of our magazine is at stake—does this story make a decided impression on you? Has it," and here I cast my eye casually at the latest announcement of a rival publication, "the kind of *tour de force* which at once excites you to the full *qui vive* and which contains a sustained *brio* that palpitates on every page? Answer carefully, Jones, because if it hasn't, I won't buy it."

"I think it has," he said.

"Very well," I answered; "now bring the author to me."

In the interval of waiting, I hastily ran my eye through the pages of the manuscript.

Presently they brought the author back again. He had assumed a look of depression.

"I have decided," I said, "to take your manuscript."

Joy broke upon his face. He came nearer to me as if to lick my hand.

"Stop a minute," I said. "I am willing to take your story, but there are certain things, certain small details which I want to change."

"Yes?" he said timidly.

"In the first place, I don't like your title. *Dorothy Dacres, or, Only a Clergyman's Daughter* is too quiet. I shall change it to read *Dorothea Dashaway, or, The Quicksands of Society.*"

"But surely," began the contributor, beginning to wring his hands——

"Don't interrupt me," I said. "In the next place, the story is much too long." Here I reached for a large pair of tailor's scissors that lay on the table. "This story contains nine thousand words. We never care to use more than six thousand. I must therefore cut some of it off." I measured the story carefully with a pocket tape that lay in front of me, cut off three thousand words and handed them back to the author. "These words," I said, "you may keep. We make no claim on them at all. You are at liberty to make any use of them that you like."

"But please," he said, "you have cut off all the end of the story: the whole conclusion is gone. The readers can't possibly tell,——"

I smiled at him with something approaching kindness.

"My dear sir," I said, "they *never* get beyond three thousand words of the end of a magazine story. The end is of no consequence whatever. The beginning, I admit, may be, but the end! Come! Come! And in any case in our magazine we print the end of each story separately, distributed among the advertisements to break the type. But just at present we have plenty of these on hand. You see," I continued, for there was something in the man's manner that almost touched me, "all that is needed is that the last words printed must have a look of finality. That's all. Now, let me see," and I turned to the place where the story was cut, "what are the last words: here: 'Dorothea sank into a chair. There we must leave her!' Excellent! What better end could you want? She sank into a chair and you leave her. Nothing more natural."

The contributor seemed about to protest. But I stopped him.

"There is one other small thing," I said. "Our coming number is to be a Plumbers' and Motor Number. I must ask you to introduce a certain amount of plumbing into your story." I rapidly turned over the pages. "I see," I said, "that your story as written is laid largely in Spain in the summer. I shall ask you to alter this to Switzerland and make it winter time to allow for the breaking of steam-pipes. Such things as these, however, are mere details; we can easily arrange them."

I reached out my hand.

"And now," I said, "I must wish you a good afternoon."

The contributor seemed to pluck up courage.

"What about remuneration"—he faltered.

I waived the question gravely aside. "You will, of course, be duly paid at our usual rate. You receive a cheque two years after publication. It will cover all your necessary expenses, including ink, paper, string, sealing-wax and other incidentals, in addition to which we hope to be able to make you a compensation for your time on a reasonable basis per hour. Good-bye."

He left, and I could hear them throwing him downstairs.

Then I sat down, while my mind was on it, and wrote the advance notice of the story. It ran like this:

NEXT MONTH'S NUMBER OF THE MEGALOMANIA MAGAZINE WILL CONTAIN A THRILLING STORY, ENTITLED

"DOROTHEA DASHAWAY, OR, THE QUICKSANDS OF SOCIETY."

The author has lately leaped into immediate recognition as the greatest master of the short story in the American World. His style has a brio, a poise, a savoir faire, a je ne sais quoi, which stamps all his work with the cachet of literary superiority. The sum paid for the story of *Dorothea Dashaway* is said to be the largest ever paid for a single MS. Every page palpitates with interest, and at the conclusion of this remarkable narrative the reader lays down the page in utter bewilderment, to turn perhaps to the almost equally marvellous illustration of Messrs. Spiggott and Fawcett's Home Plumbing Device Exposition which adorns the same number of the great review.

I wrote this out, rang the bell, and was just beginning to say to the secretary—

"My dear child,—pray pardon my forgetfulness. You must be famished for lunch. Will you permit me——"

And then I woke up—at the wrong minute, as one always does.

HOMER AND HUMBUG
AN ACADEMIC DISCUSSION

Homer and Humbug, an Academic Discussion

THE follwing discussion is of course only of interest to scholars. But, as the public schools returns show that in the United States there are now over a million coloured scholars alone, the appeal is wide enough.

I do not mind confessing that for a long time past I have been very sceptical about the classics. I was myself trained as a classical scholar. It seemed the only thing to do with me. I acquired such a singular facility in handling Latin and Greek that I could take a page of either of them, distinguish which it was by merely glancing at it, and, with the help of a dictionary and a pair of compasses, whip off a translation of it in less than three hours.

But I never got any pleasure from it. I lied about it. At first, perhaps, I lied through vanity. Any coloured scholar will understand the feeling. Later on I lied through habit; later still because, after all, the classics were all that I had and so I valued them. I have seen thus a deceived dog value a pup with a broken leg, and a pauper child nurse a dead doll with the sawdust out of it. So I nursed my dead Homer and my broken Demosthenes though I knew in my heart that there was more sawdust in the stomach of one modern author than in the whole lot of them. Observe, I am not saying which it is that has it full of it.

So, as I say, I began to lie about the classics. I said to people who knew no Greek that there was a sublimity, a majesty about Homer which they could never hope to grasp. I said it was like the sound of the sea beating against the granite cliffs of the Ionian Esophagus: or words to that effect. As for the truth of it, I might as well have said that it was like the sound of a rum distillery running a night shift on half time. At any rate this is what I said about Homer, and when I spoke of Pindar,—the dainty grace of his strophes,—and Aristophanes, the delicious sallies of his wit, sally after sally, each sally explained in a note calling it a sally—I managed to suffuse my face with an animation which made it almost beautiful.

I admitted of course that Virgil in spite of his genius had a hardness and a cold glitter which resembled rather the brilliance of a cut diamond than the soft grace of a flower. Certainly I admitted this: the mere admission of it would knock the breath out of anyone who was arguing.

From such talks my friends went away sad. The conclusion was too cruel. It had all the cold logic of a syllogism (like that almost brutal form of argument so much admired in the Paraphernalia of Socrates). For if:—

Virgil and Homer and Pindar had all this grace, and pith and these sallies,—
And if I read Virgil and Homer and Pindar,
And if they only read Mrs. Wharton and Mrs. Humphrey Ward
Then where were they?

So continued lying brought its own reward in the sense of superiority and I lied more.

When I reflect that I have openly expressed regret, as a personal matter, even in the presence of women, for the missing books of Tacitus, and the entire loss of the Abacadabra of Polyphemus of Syracuse, I can find no words in which to beg for pardon. In reality I was just as much worried over the loss of the ichthyosaurus. More, indeed: I'd like to have seen it: but if the books Tacitus lost were like those he didn't, I wouldn't.

I believe all scholars lie like this. An ancient friend of mine, a clergyman, tells me that in Hesiod he finds a peculiar grace that he doesn't find elsewhere. He's a liar. That's all. Another man, in politics and in the legislature, tells me that every night before going to bed he reads over a page or two of Thucydides to keep his mind fresh. Either he never goes to bed or he's a liar. Doubly so: no one could read Greek at that frantic rate: and anyway his mind isn't fresh. How could it be, he's in the legislature. I don't object to this man talking freely of the classics, but he ought to keep it for the voters. My own opinion is that before he goes to bed he takes whiskey: why call it Thucydides?

I know there are solid arguments advanced in favour of the classics. I often hear them from my colleagues. My friend the professor of Greek tells me that he truly believes the classics have made him what he is. This is a very grave statement, if well founded. Indeed I have heard the same argument from a great many Latin and Greek scholars. They all claim, with some heat, that Latin and Greek have practically made them what they are. This damaging charge against the classics should not be too readily accepted. In my opinion some of these men would have been what they are, no matter what they were.

Be this as it may, I for my part bitterly regret the lies I have told about my appreciation of Latin and Greek literature. I am anxious to do what I can to set things right. I am therefore engaged on, indeed have nearly completed, a work which will enable all readers to judge the matter for themselves. What I have done is a translation of all the great classics, not in the usual literal way but on a design that brings them into harmony with modern life. I will explain what I mean in a minute.

The translation is intended to be within reach of everybody. It is so designed that the entire set of volumes can go on a shelf twenty-seven feet long, or even longer. The first edition will be an *édition de luxe* bound in vellum, or perhaps in buckskin, and sold at five hundred dollars. It will be limited to five hundred copies and, of course, sold only to the feeble minded. The next edition will be the Literary Edition, sold to artists, authors, actors and contractors. After that will come the Boarding House Edition, bound in board and paid for in the same way.

My plan is to so transpose the classical writers as to give, not the literal translation word for word, but what is really the modern equivalent. Let me give an odd sample or two to show what I mean. Take the passage in the First Book of Homer that describes Ajax the Greek dashing into the battle in front of Troy. Here is the way it runs (as nearly as I remember), in the usual word for word translation of the classroom, as done by the very best professor, his spectacles glittering with the literary rapture of it.

"Then he too Ajax on the one hand leaped (or possibly jumped) into the fight wearing on the other hand, yes certainly a steel corselet (or possibly a bronze under tunic) and on his head of course, yes without doubt he had a helmet with a tossing plume taken from the mane (or perhaps extracted from the tail) of some horse which once fed along the banks of the Scamander (and it sees the herd and raises its head and paws the ground) and in his hand a shield worth a hundred oxen and on his knees too especially in particular greaves made by some cunning artificer (or perhaps blacksmith) and he blows the fire and it is hot. Thus Ajax leapt (or, better, was propelled from behind), into the fight."

Now that's grand stuff. There is no doubt of it. There's a wonderful movement and force to it. You can almost see it move, it goes so fast. But the modern reader can't get it. It won't mean to him what it meant to the early Greek. The setting, the costume, the scene has all got to be changed in order to let the reader have a real equivalent to judge just how good the Greek verse is. In my translation I alter it just a little, not much but just enough to give the passage a form that reproduces the proper literary value of the verses, without losing anything of the majesty. It describes, I may say, the Directors of the American Industrial Stocks rushing into the Balkan War Cloud.—

> Then there came rushing to the shock of war
> Mr. McNicoll of the C. P. R.
> He wore suspenders and about his throat
> High rose the collar of a sealskin coat.
> He had on gaiters and he wore a tie,
> He had his trousers buttoned good and high;
> About his waist a woollen undervest
> Bought from a sad-eyed farmer of the West.
> (And every time he clips a sheep he sees
> Some bloated plutocrat who ought to freeze),
> Thus in the Stock Exchange he burst to view,
> Leaped to the post, and shouted, "Ninety-two!"

There! That's Homer, the real thing! Just as it sounded to the rude crowd of Greek peasants who sat in a ring and guffawed at the rhymes and watched the minstrel stamp it out into "feet" as he recited it!

Or let me take another example from the so-called Catalogue of the Ships that fills up nearly an entire book of Homer. This famous passage names all the ships, one by one, and names the chiefs who sailed on them, and names the particular town or hill or valley that they came from. It has been much admired. It has that same majesty of style that has been brought to an even loftier pitch in the New York Business Directory and the City Telephone Book. It runs along, as I recall it, something like this,—

"And first, indeed, oh yes, was the ship of Homistogetes the Spartan, long and swift, having both its masts covered with cowhide and two rows of oars. And he, Homistogetes, was born of Hermogenes and Ophthalmia and was at home in Syncope beside the fast flowing Paresis. And after him came the ship of Preposterus the Eurasian, son of Oasis and Hyteria," . . . and so on endlessly.

Instead of this I substitute, with the permission of the New York Central Railway, the official catalogue of their locomotives taken almost word for word from the list compiled by their superintendent of works. I admit that he wrote in hot weather. Part of it runs:—

Out in the yard and steaming in the sun
Stands locomotive engine number forty-one;
Seated beside the windows of the cab
Are Pat McGaw and Peter James McNab.
Pat comes from Troy and Peter from Cohoes,
And when they pull the throttle off she goes;
And as she vanishes there comes to view
Steam locomotive engine number forty-two.
Observe her mighty wheels, her easy roll,
With William J. Macarthy in control.
They say her engineer some time ago
Lived on a farm outside of Buffalo
Whereas his fireman, Henry Edward Foy,
Attended School in Springfield, Illinois.
Thus does the race of man decay or rot—
Some men can hold their jobs and some can not.

Please observe that if Homer had actually written that last line it would have been quoted for a thousand years as one of the deepest sayings ever said. Orators would have rounded out their speeches with the majestic phrase, quoted in sonorous and unintelligible Greek verse, "some men can hold their jobs and some can not": essayists would have begun their most scholarly dissertations with the words,—"It has been finely said by Homer that (in Greek) 'some men can hold their jobs'": and the clergy in mid-pathos of a funeral sermon would have raised their eyes aloft and echoed "Some men can not"!

This is what I should like to do. I'd like to take a large stone and write on it in very plain writing,—

"The classics are only primitive literature. They belong in the same class as primitive machinery and primitive music and primitive medicine,"—and then throw it through the windows of a University and hide behind a fence to see the professors buzz!!